Bond

The secrets of
Writing

Michellejoy Hughes

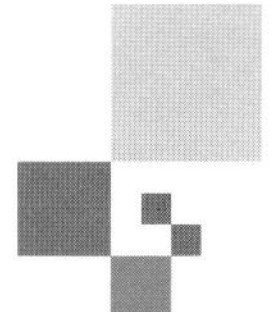

Nelson Thornes

Published in 2009 by:
Nelson Thornes Ltd
Delta Place
27 Bath Road
CHELTENHAM
GL53 7TH
United Kingdom

11 12 13 / 10 9 8 7 6 5 4

A catalogue record for this book is available from the British Library

ISBN 978 0 7487 8481 3

Illustrations by Fakenham Photosetting Limited
Page make-up by Fakenham Photosetting Limited, Norfolk

Photograph acknowledgements
iStockphoto p79
Michellejoy Hughes p24a, p24b, p84

Printed and bound in Croatia by Zrinski

Contents

A Introduction

1 Why do you need this book?

Writing remains a central aspect of literacy teaching in schools but many children still struggle with developing this vital life skill. The ability to write at an early age underpins not only specific writing exams taken within school, but also forms the basis for their future written communication skills.

This book is therefore an invaluable resource for all children, from the beginning of Year 3 through to the end of Year 9, as it covers the writing requirements for the 11^+, 12^+ and 13^+ exams, the Common Entrance Examination, the Key Stage 2 English SATs and the Key Stage 3 English Assessments. These exams are explained in more detail below. It is also a useful manual that can support school-based learning and can provide additional help for anyone who wants to improve his or her writing skills.

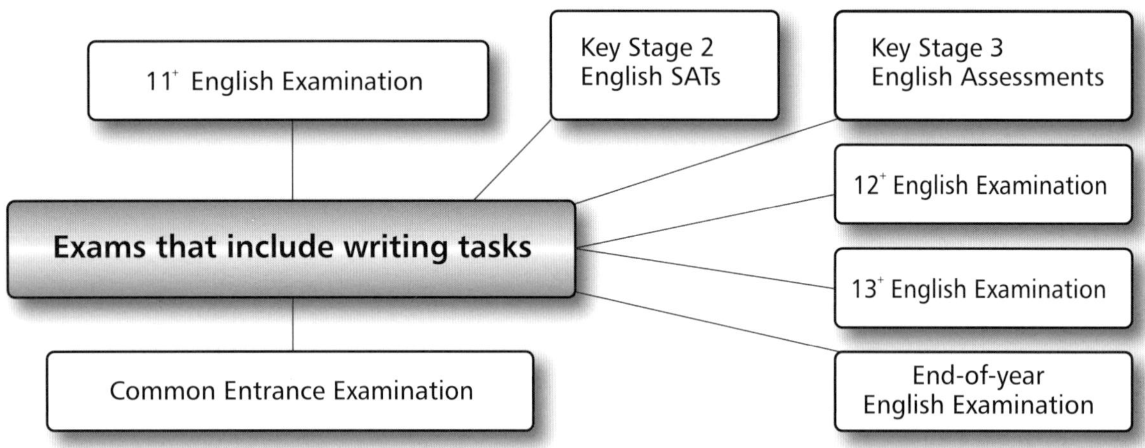

The 11^+ Examination is a test used by UK grammar schools and some selective secondary schools to assess the academic ability of pupils who are applying to join the school in the following September. An 11^+ exam can test some or all of a child's English, maths, verbal and non-verbal reasoning skills in individual subject papers, which can be written in a standard or multiple-choice format.

Most 11^+ English exams include at least one writing task. This may form a section within a combined English paper that tests comprehension, writing, spelling, grammar and punctuation skills, or a separate writing paper may be set. Some schools will set a writing task, although it may not be marked unless a child's total is borderline with the qualifying score. Other schools may only consider writing tasks in the event of an appeal by parents, if their child has been initially unsuccessful in gaining entry to the school.

Where the writing task is taken into account for the overall English score, it can carry up to 50% of the available marks. Usually a child has to choose one or two questions to answer from a selection of options. Questions can be based on a wide range of themes or writing styles to test a child's skills, for example: a factual essay or description; a piece of fictional narrative or descriptive writing; a formal/informal letter or diary entry; a debate; a continuation of a piece of given text; or a composition based on a visual stimulus such as a photograph.

Whatever format a writing task may take, it usually tests a pupil's ability to clearly organise ideas, write an appropriate and focused answer, engage the reader and use accurate elements of spelling, grammar, punctuation and sentence structure. Depending on whether the writing task is an element of a combined paper, or whether a separate writing paper is set, the time limit can be anywhere between 30 minutes and 1 hour 15 minutes (including reading and planning time).

The time of year when these exams are taken can differ from region to region, but most schools and/or LAs set them between September and January. Always find out from a school when their exam is being set, what subjects are being tested and in what format the exam papers are written.

The 12$^+$ and 13$^+$ Examinations form part of the late transfer process for some grammar and selective secondary schools. These exams are used to assess the ability of a small number of pupils who may apply to join the school in Years 8 or 9. The format and skills tested are similar to those in the 11$^+$ exams, though the content is likely to be more advanced at this stage.

As for the 11$^+$, the writing task(s) may form a section within a combined test or a separate paper may be set. The format of the tasks will also be similar to those found in the 11$^+$ but, at this level, the expectations of the examiner will be higher. A more accurate and in-depth level of word knowledge, spellings, grammar usage and overall writing style will be required.

The Common Entrance Examination (CEE) is used by many independent schools to assess pupils who are transferring to a secondary school at the age of 11 or 13. The 11$^+$ level exam is sat during the spring school term, whereas the 13$^+$ level exam can be sat in either the spring or the summer term. The three core subjects of English, maths and science are tested at both entrance levels.

A writing paper will usually be included in both English exams. At 11$^+$ level, pupils will usually be asked to choose one prompt to write about from a range of four to six options (based on similar formats to those listed for the 11$^+$ above) and will be marked on elements of content, purpose, style, organisation and breadth of vocabulary. Additional marks will be awarded for correct use of grammar, punctuation, spelling and presentation (handwriting).

For the 13$^+$ exam, pupils often have to complete two writing tasks; one based on a theme relating to a text they have previously read, the second a piece of creative writing. A choice of prompts is usually given for both tasks and marks are awarded in a similar way to the 11$^+$ level task.

At 11$^+$ entry level, around 40 minutes (plus a few minutes reading and planning time) will be given for the writing task, whereas both tasks in the 13$^+$ exam must be completed in around 1 hour 20 minutes (including time to read and plan). For both levels, the writing tasks are likely to carry 50% of the total English marks, the remaining 50% being taken from a comprehension paper.

Standard Attainment Tests (SATs) are the compulsory exams sat at the end of
Key Stage 2, although some schools do use optional SATs in other years. They are
government-set requirements that test pupils in English, maths and science. In the
English SATs, the writing element is presented in the form of a short task and a long
task.

Around 20 minutes is usually set for the short task and the longer task, often a piece
of non-fiction writing or a story, must be planned and completed within 45 minutes.
For these tasks, a choice of starting points may not be given but planning templates are
provided to help children organise their ideas quickly. As for the exams listed above,
children are marked on their ability to write well, engage the reader, use punctuation
accurately and include a range of vocabulary. The presentation of their text (their
handwriting) is assessed in the longer writing task.

Key Stage 3 teacher assessments comprise a range of tasks and tests that are set
by individual teachers in a range of foundation subjects (such as English, maths and
science) throughout the key stage. Although the formats of these assessments may differ,
each test and task is designed to help a teacher track a child's progress against the
national curriculum attainment targets. By the end of key stage 3, children are expected
to have achieved level 5 in all core subjects.

For a child to reach this level in their writing, they must consistently produce material
that, for example, is varied and interesting; conveys meaning clearly in a range of
different formats and for different readers; shows a broad and imaginative vocabulary;
demonstrates accurate usage of simple and complex sentences that are structured in
clear, well-organised paragraphs; shows accurate use of a wide range of punctuation;
demonstrates sound spelling knowledge; and is presented in a clear, fluent and joined
handwriting style.

End-of-year exams may be independently set by individual schools, but it is now quite
common for schools to buy in government SATs for non-compulsory years (Years 3, 4,
5, 7 and 8). Whether a school uses their own end-of-year exams or uses SATs, there will
usually be at least one writing task in the English paper. These exams are designed to
test the same skills as the compulsory SATs papers, so they often present tasks in similar
formats and follow a common marking scheme.

2   How can you use this book?

The secrets of Writing is a practical guide designed for use by children, but it features
tips and advice for parents too. It makes clear the skills needed to produce effective,
engaging pieces of writing and highlights ways in which parents can help their children
to strengthen these skills. This book is full of practical techniques and exercises that
cover the main elements of both factual and fictional writing and it offers help for all
ages and abilities.

Strong writing skills form the basis for so many exams where children need to express
themselves. This book can therefore be used to support writing skills for all cross-
curricular subjects where writing tasks form an element of assessment. As all core stages
of writing are explored, from choosing a question prompt and generating creative ideas,
through to planning and presentation, *The secrets of Writing* will also help to build a

sound foundation upon which practice for more advanced writing tasks, such as for GCSE English, can be based.

This key resource is part of the long-established Bond series, which continues to be used by many parents and tutors to help children prepare for the 11[+] (or other selective entry exams), as well as to support practice for SATs, teacher assessments and general skills improvement. Using this handbook in conjunction with the other English resources in the series will help to provide a wide variety of practice for writing skills. Details of the full range of Bond English resources available are listed in the Additional resources appendix in section C.

3 How is this book organised?

This book is divided into three main sections:

A *Introduction*
B *Three steps to successful writing*
C *Appendices*

Section A explains the stages when children are likely to face writing tests between Year 3 and Year 9, which skills will be tested in these exams, and how you can support and develop your child's ability.

Section B contains the core content of the book, taking children steadily through three key steps to help them improve their writing skills.

1 Understand the task
Here children will see how to choose the question that will best show off their writing skills; study examples of different styles of writing prompt; discover tips on how to recognise each type of question; understand the key facts that they should consider about each type of writing task; and learn the difference between some common writing styles.

2 Improve your writing
This next step takes a detailed look at the ways in which children can develop their writing by: providing three detailed techniques that they can use to generate a wide range of creative ideas; explaining the importance of planning and offering a suggested method for producing a detailed plan for each of the core types of writing prompt; exploring a broad range of ways in which they can enhance the quality of what they write; highlighting the importance of what their writing actually looks like; and encouraging them to think about how fast they can produce their work. Practice activities are included throughout so that children can not only read about the different techniques but they can also try them for themselves. Where the icon www is shown next to a practice activity, this indicates that a sample answer is available free to download from our website. Children may find it helpful to compare these examples to their answers for these activities. To access these samples, visit www.bond11plus.co.uk and follow the Free Resources link for this book.

3 Boost the basics
This section gives children a brief but important reminder of the key roles of spelling, grammar and punctuation in writing. Spelling skills are supported by several essential

strategies and tips, while knowledge of the core elements of grammar and punctuation are tested through quizzes. Sources of further help on any of these aspects are also suggested.

Section C provides details of the additional English resources that you can use alongside this book, whether your child needs support for selective secondary school entrance exams, English SATs, teacher assessments or general improvement of basic English skills. Short answers to certain tasks given throughout the book can be found here (also see above for details of online sample answers). Details of the online extracts that relate to some practice activities are also listed here.

4 What skills will your child need?

As we have seen, children need to use their writing skills throughout their education and in particular for tests that include specific writing assessment tasks. These tests may be set at different difficulty levels but each task will be testing a similar set of skills. In all of these tests, examiners will be looking for children to display ability in key areas and to meet particular learning targets.

By the time of the 11$^+$, your child will be expected to show that he or she can:

- *write imaginatively in a range of forms (narrative, playscript, report or opinion, for example)*
- *adapt writing to suit the task, purpose and reader*
- *understand what tone is required*
- *recognise the difference between formal and informal writing tasks*
- *use different narrative techniques to engage, entertain and communicate, developing writing that:*
  - *explores feelings and experiences*
  - *informs, explains and describes*
  - *persuades, advises and argues*
  - *reviews, analyses and comments*
- *understand the differences between writing Standard and non-Standard English*
- *draw on an extended vocabulary and use it inventively*
- *use all parts of speech accurately (such as noun/verb agreements, adjectives, adverbs, conjunctions, prepositions and dialogue)*
- *construct sentences in different ways to ensure clarity, express meaning and create effects*
- *use punctuation marks correctly in different sentence types*
- *structure simple and complex sentences*
- *organise and develop ideas effectively*
- *write in a logical and structured way, using paragraphs*
- *plan, draft and revise writing*
- *spell accurately, for example:*
  - *apply knowledge of spelling conventions and exceptions (such as word roots, letter strings, prefixes)*
  - *use spelling strategies to spell difficult or unfamiliar words*
- *write fluently, at speed and at reasonable length on a particular topic*

- *write legibly in joined and printed handwriting styles*
- *adapt handwriting for specific purposes (such as print for diagram labels, note taking for rough draft and longhand for neat work).*

These key skills are central to the 11[+], 12[+] and 13[+] exams, the CEE and the English SATs and teacher assessments, so it is important for your child to feel confident in every one of these areas.

5   How can you help?

Before your child begins this handbook, and while he or she works through it, there are many ways in which you can support and improve your child's aptitude for writing. Here are a range of practical ideas that you can try with your child.

Widen your child's exposure to writing and story-telling by:

- *keeping a well-stocked bookshelf*
- *encouraging them to talk about books*
- *re-reading favourite stories together*
- *visiting your local library or book shop*
- *playing story tapes at home or in the car*
- *taking them to the theatre*
- *using toys or puppets to act out scenes*
- *checking if your child's favourite film or television series is based on a book*
- *encouraging them to add their own reviews to relevant online blogs*
- *increasing your stock of comics and magazines*
- *visiting a literary festival.*

✓ **Parent Tip**

Try writing some short stories or letters yourself and then share them with your child. Talk about elements such as the structure, tone, aim and purpose, reader, plot ideas, effects used and so on. Or start them off with a paragraph or two and see how they finish the piece of creative writing.

Encourage high-quality content and presentation by:

- *developing word knowledge*
- *promoting Standard English*
- *using a stop watch. As with all exams, writing tasks will be timed. It is therefore important to practice writing at speed*
- *supporting handwriting skills*
- *highlighting the importance of checking.*

✓ Parent Tip

Exam instructions may ask for answers to be written in either pen or pencil, so it is useful for your child to be familiar with both types of writing implement.

Create a positive writing environment by:

- *giving your child the opportunity to write in different locations*
- *displaying examples of their writing*
- *making time to read or listen to your child's compositions*
- *discussing topics that matter to them*
- *suggesting opportunities for their work to be 'published'. For example, in a school magazine, or as part of a writing competition.*

✓ Parent Tip

If your child is a slow reader, they may read the words on a page but actually gain little or no understanding from them. This in turn will provide little motivation for them to persevere with their reading. Try reading a section of text aloud first, so that your child gains the gist of the text, and then let them read the same section back to you. By creating a dramatic atmosphere through your tone of voice (exaggerated punctuation, a voice for different characters, etc.), you can provide a template for their own interpretations. When your child completes a piece of writing, encourage them to give the reader 'interpretation tips' (detailed descriptions, clear dialogue and so on). Read their writing back to them and always ask if they are happy with the result or if they think they can improve it. Helping your child to understand this link between reading and writing is crucial to their literacy development.

As writing skills underpin many other subjects, success in this area can affect your child's performance across the broader curriculum. The information and exercises that follow show children what they should be looking out for in any writing test, as well as strategies for improving their skills.

Writing tasks will form a key element of several compulsory English exams that you will take, from Year 1 tests and assessments through to GCSE English. Several test papers may instruct you to answer one question from a selection of options but for others you may have to complete more than one task in the given time frame. This may involve writing one factual piece of text and one creative, fictional piece to show your aptitude for different writing styles.

The length of, or word limit for, writing tasks can also differ. Often it depends on the type of task and writing guidelines will frequently be given. These can range from requesting two or three paragraphs (about 250 words) for short answers to one or two sides of A4 paper for more detailed tasks. The length of a piece of writing might also depend on the size of a pupil's handwriting or how much they can think to write.

Writing tasks are often based on a wide range of themes or styles in order to test a variety of skills. For example, a task could take the form of a factual essay or description, a piece of fictional narrative, a formal/informal letter or diary entry, a continuation of a piece of given text or a composition based on a visual stimulus such as a photograph.

Whatever form a task might take, there are common writing problems that many children struggle with and under exam conditions these problems are often magnified. In timed tests, many capable pupils can easily lose precious marks. This book will help you to develop the skills needed to confidently complete a range of writing tasks. It will show you how to:

- *choose a question*
- *think up lots of ideas and plan different tasks*
- *develop the quality and presentation of your writing*
- *increase your speed*
- *boost your spelling, grammar and punctuation.*

Working through this book will help you to feel comfortable and confident with each of the skills you will need, ensuring that you have the best possible grounding for writing tasks.

1 Understand the task

Choose the question

Usually a writing paper will give you the option of choosing one or two writing tasks out of a set of title prompts, though you may not always be given an option. If you do have a choice of titles, how do you choose which one(s) to write about? Often, children are tempted to choose the first writing prompt they read but this may not always be the best option. Think about your strengths in writing and ask yourself some questions as you read through the options. For example:

- *Do you find it easier to create fictional or factual pieces of writing?*
- *Do you prefer writing within a given structure or do you like being fully creative?*
- *Do you find pictures or images a helpful starting point for ideas?*
- *Can you bring your favourite book, poem or play to mind quickly?*
- *Does a title remind you of a recent event or situation that you can recall quite clearly?*
- *How much time do you have for the task(s)? Is there a question that you think will be more straightforward to answer in the time frame?*

Thinking about questions like these should help you to narrow down the set of options, making it easier to choose between them. Once you have chosen a title prompt, there is one more check you can do to confirm that your chosen option will show your writing skills at their best. During the planning stage (see section B2, 'Create a plan'), think about whether you have been able to note down several key points to include in your answer. If you haven't been able to think of many, then it might be better to choose a different question.

So what types of writing prompts could you have to choose between?

Many question types will be based around your imagination and originality. For example, a prompt could take the form of a:

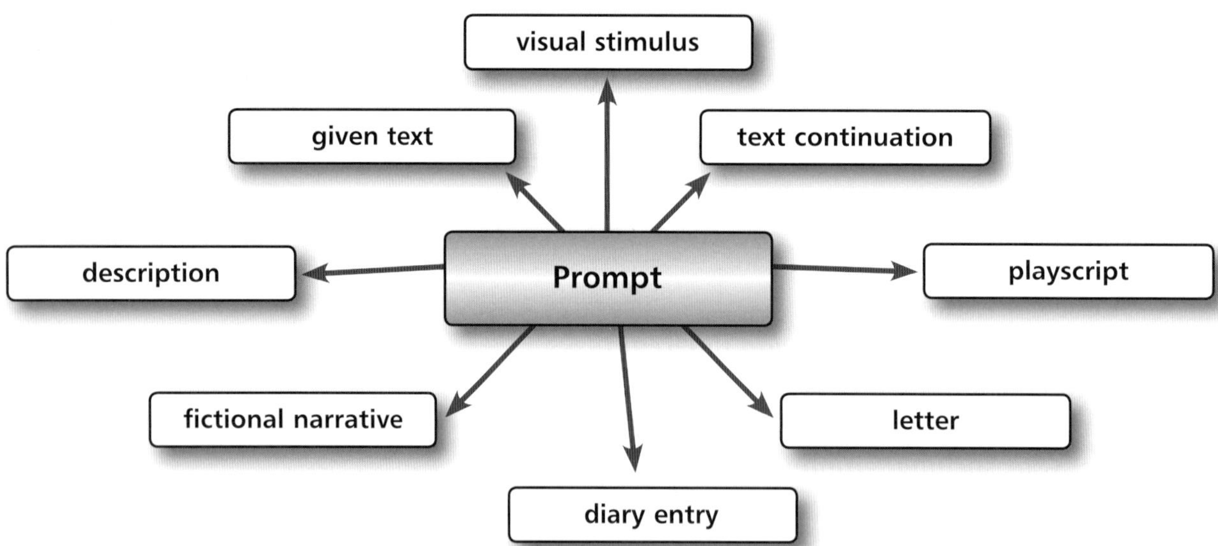

Other questions will require you to draw on your existing knowledge as well as your analysis skills and personal opinion. For example:

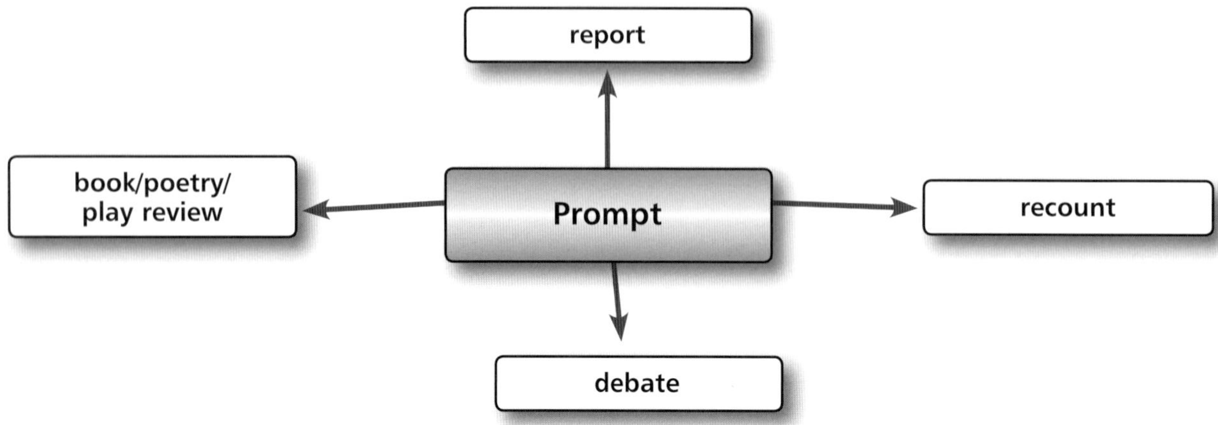

Depending on the theme of a question, your response to some composition titles, such as those requiring a report, recount, description or fictional narrative, could be based completely on fact, totally on fiction, or a combination of both.

Writing prompts can be based on many different themes or writing styles so it is important for you to recognise what *type* of question you have chosen. At the same time, in order to be awarded high marks, you need to be familiar with the literary elements and style of writing that your answer should follow. The following sections should help you to recall the key points about a wide range of writing formats.

● Recognise the format

As you may be asked to write in a variety of formats, it is important to recognise what the typical elements of each format are so that you can write convincingly. Let's have a closer look at some of the most common formats that were shown above.

(a) *Letter prompts*

A letter prompt is a very common question type that is normally easy to identify in a set of options, as the question instruction will usually include the word 'letter' or a phrase that implies writing to someone. Prompts often give you guidelines on the core points you should cover in your answer. For example:

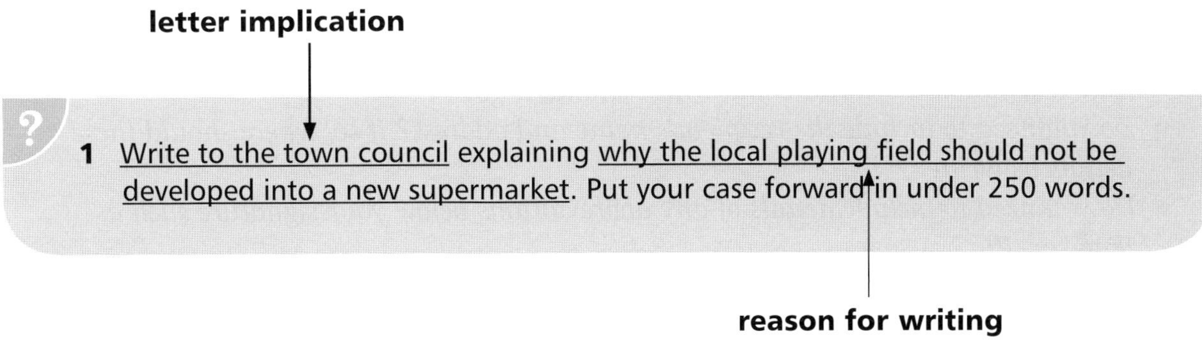

You may feel that choosing a letter is a relatively straightforward option as the base for your answer is likely to be outlined in the question. Although this provides a useful guide for the content, there are still a number of key elements you need to consider and questions that you need to ask yourself when drafting a letter.

Firstly, you will need to think about who you are writing to. The intended reader will determine whether you need to write in a formal or informal style and this, in turn, will have an impact on the style of greeting, tone, layout and structure of the letter:

- *Will your letter start with a formal greeting like: 'Dear Sir/Madam'; 'To the Editor'; or an informal greeting like: 'Hello! How are you?'; 'Hi!'?*
- *Should the tone be firm and direct or chatty and relaxed?*
- *Will each set of points need to be organised clearly in short, separate paragraphs or can all of the content be written in one paragraph?*
- *Should your letter end with a phrase such as: 'Yours sincerely'; 'Yours faithfully'; or 'Bye for now'; 'Take care'; 'Love and best wishes'?*
- *Should you sign your name in the style of 'Mr Philip Hughes' or 'Phil'?*

You will then need to think carefully about the purpose of the letter. Look back at the question prompt for clues about why you are writing. Are you explaining, recounting, arranging, enquiring or complaining about something? Again, the aim of your letter will influence what you write and how you write it.

Lastly, consider the basic style points for all letters:

- *What position should your name and address details be placed in?*
- *How will you write the date and where should it go?*
- *Do you need to include the recipient's name and address? If so, where should these details be written?*
- *Do you need to include details of any abbreviations below your signature such as 'Enc.' or 'P.S.'?*

www   Now it's your turn!

Practise your letter writing skills by choosing one of the question prompts above and completing the task in your notebook. Think about how your letter addresses the key points raised in this section before asking someone to comment on your work.

 **Top Tip**

For guidance on planning letters see pages 67–71. You will also find some useful tips on writing formal and informal letters in *Bond How to do ... 11+ English*, section C7 and *The secrets of Comprehension*, section B1: 'Recognise different text types'. (See the Additional resources appendix in section C for details.)

ⓑ *Diary prompts*

A diary prompt is another type of question that should be quite easy to identify amongst a set of options. Often this style of prompt will include the term 'diary', although sometimes writing a diary entry may be implied in the question rather than being specifically stated. It is also usually possible to work out some of the core points that should be covered, as well as the perspective from which the entry should be written. For example:

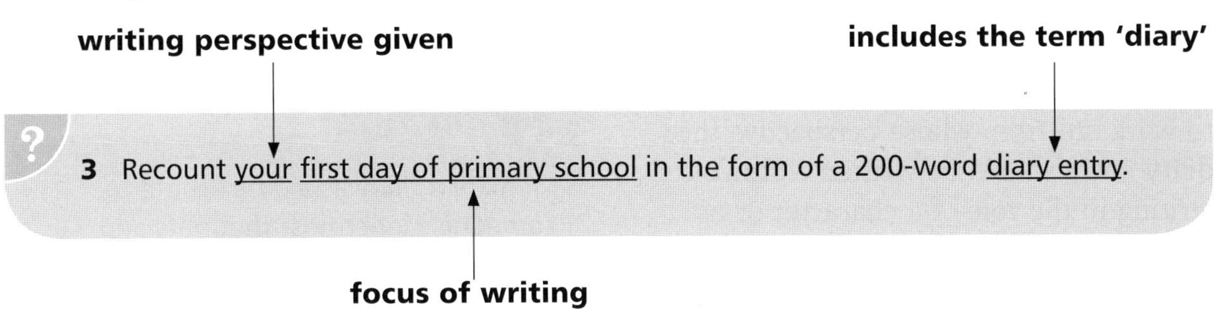

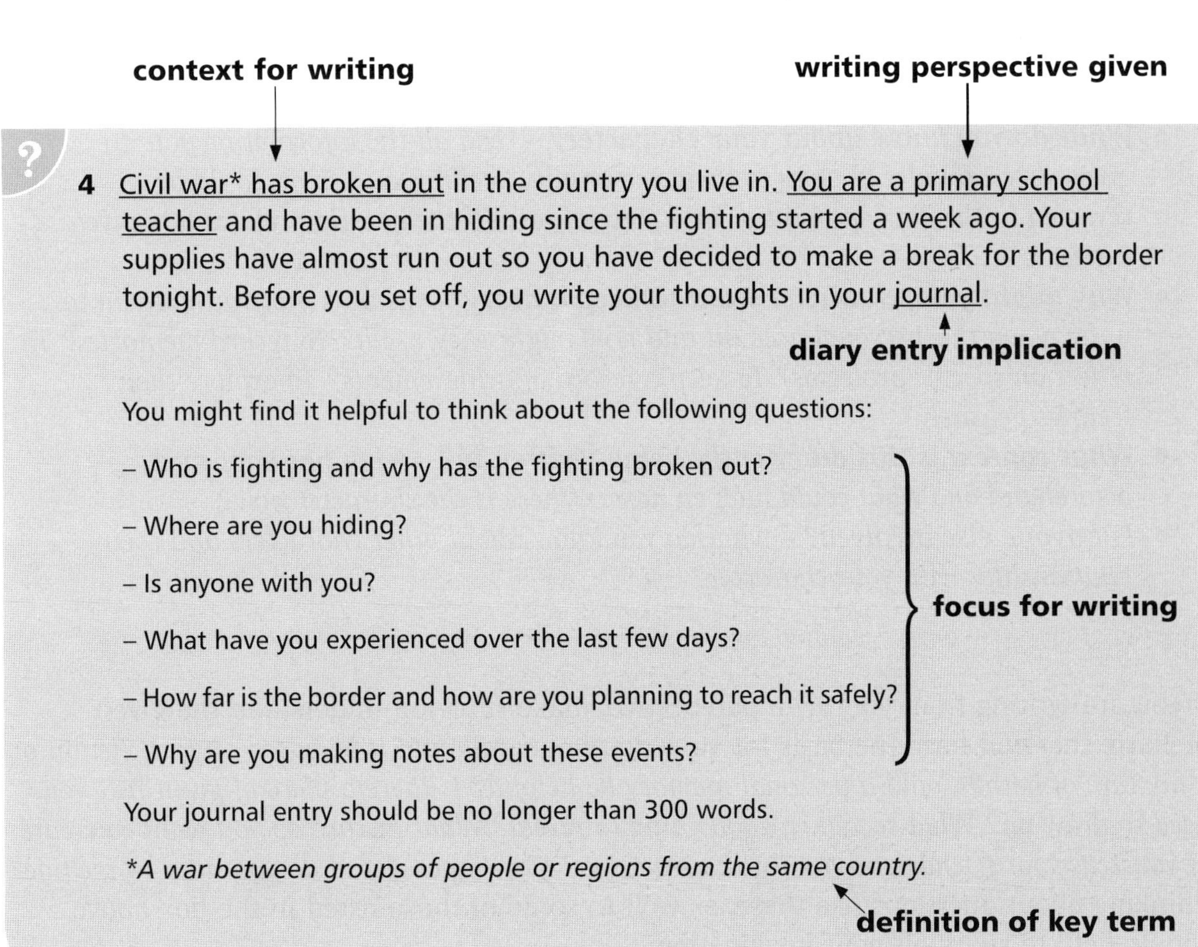

This type of writing prompt may seem like a straightforward option but there are several key points that you should consider, as well as particular rules you need to remember, when preparing to write a diary entry.

Firstly, think about what makes up a diary. A diary is a collection of recount writing but diary entries are different to other styles of recounts. A diary is usually thought of as 'secret' so, unlike other types of recounts such as formal reports, the information it contains is not meant to be read by anyone except the writer. As a result, these recounts can be very emotional and reveal a lot about the writer but they can also contain bias and present a subjective view of events.

Next, look carefully at the question prompts to work out from whose perspective the diary entry should be written – are you writing in the role of a character or as yourself? It can be difficult to see yourself in the role of another person so, if you are writing as a particular character, try to answer some key questions such as:

Think of a diary as a direct route to someone's innermost thoughts and feelings – a place where they can secretly reflect on specific events, situations, people, relationships and so on.

- *What do you know about your character? – read all the information you are given very carefully as clues to their personality, feelings and so on could be revealed in the diary prompt or in a piece of text (if the question relates to a given extract).*
- *Why might your character want to keep a diary? – what is motivating them to write down this personal account and how might they use it? To record memories? To reflect on specific problems? To keep a record of achievements? To explore their feelings privately?*
- *What context is this diary entry being written in? – what has happened beforehand and what could happen next? Where is the character now?*
- *Is anyone else involved? – what do you know about other characters and their relationships with your character?*

If you are writing from your own perspective, make sure you understand the given scenario that will form the basis for your diary entry. *Should it be based on fact, fiction or a mixture of both? Could a personal memory be helpful? Is there a piece of given text you need to draw on? What secrets are you going to reveal? What picture do you want to create of yourself, your friends and family, the situation? How much detail do you need to include?* Thinking about questions like these, as well as some of those listed in the box above, should help to spark off your imagination.

Finally, consider the basic writing conventions.

Key Facts

Diary entries:

- often open with a greeting, e.g. 'Dear Diary'
- show the date at the top
- should be written in the first person
- should be written in a chatty, lively, informal writing style
- should reveal intimate details of the writer's thoughts and feelings
- are usually written in the past tense unless the writer is commenting on future events
- often include elements of reported speech (not direct speech)
- recount events in chronological order
- should be organised into paragraphs
- use conjunctions and time connectives to link from one point to the next
- often finish with a closing statement or 'sign off', e.g. *It's late, so I'll say goodnight and tell you more tomorrow, J.*

 Now it's your turn!

Practise your diary writing skills by choosing one of the question prompts above and completing the task in your notebook. Think about how your diary entry addresses the key points raised in this section before asking someone to comment on your work.

Top Tip

Why not try keeping a diary? You could use it to record your adventures and achievements as well as note down your thoughts and feelings.

 **Parent Tip**

To familiarise children with the writing style and topics that can be covered by diaries, try reading some published (fictional and factual) diaries together, e.g. The **My Story** series, **The Diary of the Killer Cat** and **Jennifer's Diary** by Anne Fine; the **Dolphin Diaries** series by Lucy Daniels; the **Dear Dumb Diary** series by Jim Benton; **The Diary of Anne Frank** and **Zlata's Diary**.

(c) *Fictional narrative prompts*

Fictional narrative prompts are usually quite easy to spot in a set of options as they often include the term 'story' or imply that a piece of creative writing is required – either through the phrasing of the question or the writing topic. They require imagination as they are frequently based on scenarios that are unlikely or impossible in reality. They often provide very little guidance, giving you only a title and possibly a guide on length. Here are two examples:

implication of creative writing   **writing topic suggests fictional narrative**

5 Write creatively about the following title: 'A week in the life of an orange'. Write up to two sides of A4 paper.

includes the term 'story'   **writing topic suggests fictional narrative**

6 Write a 250-word story entitled: 'The Day I Met the Queen'.

This type of writing prompt may seem like an appealing option because it allows you to draw heavily on your imagination but, for questions where little guidance on content or structure is given, it can be difficult to know where to start.

The key to fictional narratives is to try and generate your own set of points to consider, as these can form the basis of your writing. An effective way of doing this is to 'interview' yourself. For example, here are some basic interview questions and answers that you might think about in response to question prompt 6 above:

- *Who are you?*   *My name is Emily and I'm a fashion designer.*
- *Where are you?*   *I'm in Buckingham Palace.*
- *Why are you there?*   *My design idea won a fashion competition.*
- *What are you doing?*   *I'm waiting to show the Queen the final design I have created for her charity ball dress.*
- *How are you doing it?*   *I have brought my design folder with me and several swatches of material that she can choose from.*

Remember that the questions and answers you note down must relate in some way to the context given in the title or question prompt. It is easy to lose direction when you let your imagination loose! Once you have some basic ideas about the given topic, you can use them as a springboard for your writing.

When completing a piece of creative, fictional narrative, it is also a good idea to check that you are:

- writing in continuous text
- following a clear plot line and structure: beginning, middle, end
- organising your points into paragraphs
- introducing characters as and when appropriate
- clear about who is narrating and writing in the correct voice: first, second, third person
- including enough detail to keep your reader entertained
- including any relevant writing style principles: e.g. a thriller or adventure story can build up tension through short sentences; a descriptive narration is likely to draw on the reader's senses to help them engage with the plot
- showing the full breadth of your vocabulary knowledge
- using correct grammar, spelling and punctuation
- including direct or reported speech as needed
- leading up to an appropriate ending: a moral, a learning point, or a resolution to a climax for example, try to avoid the 'it was all a dream' style of ending.

Thinking about points like these will make sure that your writing addresses the key elements of any piece of fictional narrative.

Even if a writing prompt states that you do not have to write a complete story or piece of creative, fictional writing, the extract that you write must still follow a logical path and come to an appropriate stopping point.

www Now it's your turn!

Practise your fictional narrative writing skills by choosing one of the question prompts above and completing the task in your notebook. Think about how your fictional narrative addresses the key points raised in this section before asking someone to comment on your work.

A text continuation prompt is a common question type that is normally easy to identify. The question instruction is likely to include a few sentences of opening text or it may refer you back to a piece of text previously seen in an earlier reading task. This style of prompt will often give you guidelines on the core points you should cover in your answer. For example:

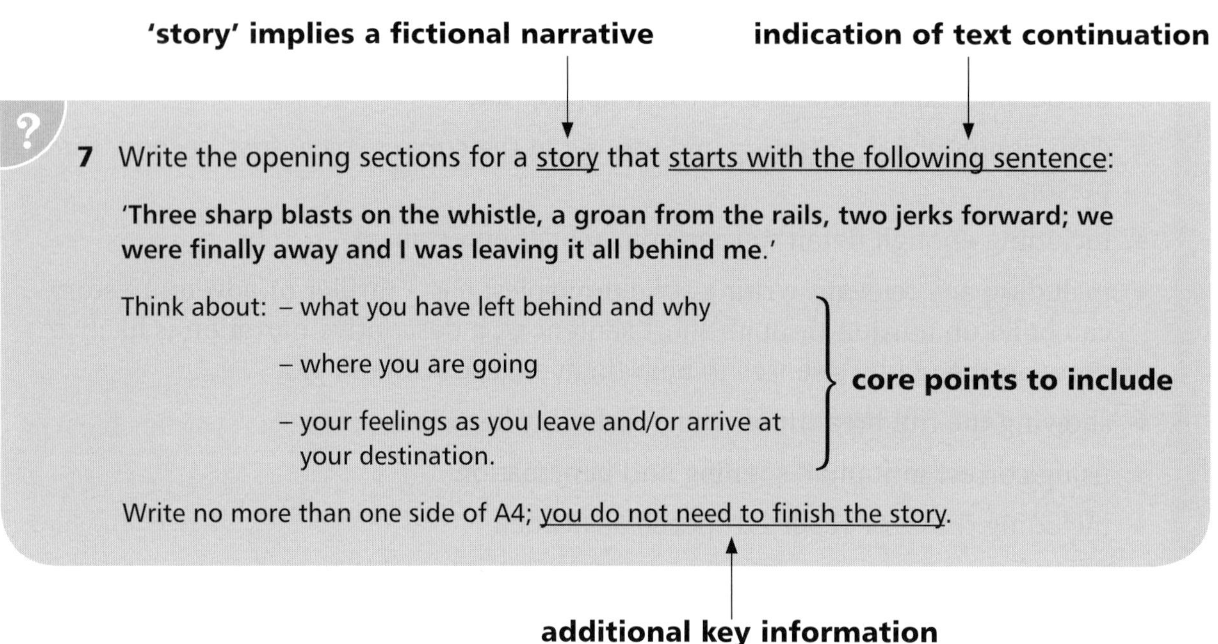

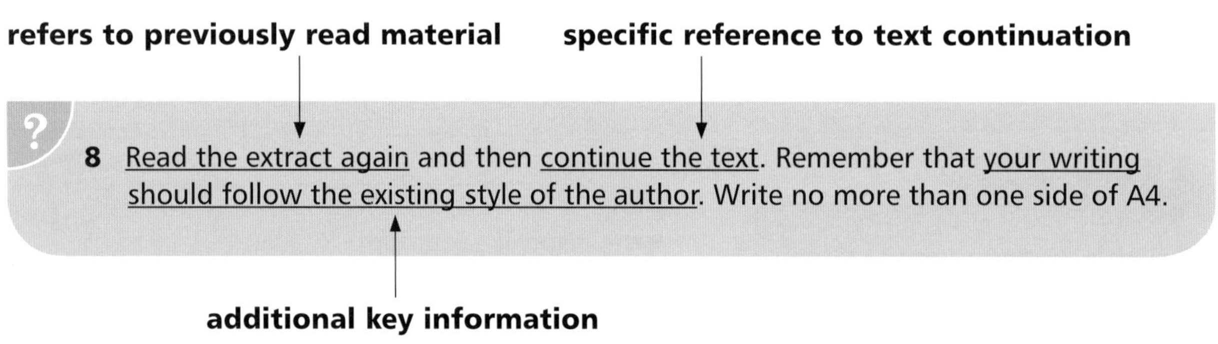

You may feel that choosing a text continuation is a relatively straightforward option as the base for your answer has already been set out in the question. Although the text that is provided is a useful starting point, there are still a number of key elements you need to consider and questions you need to ask yourself when continuing a text. For example:

- *Does it remind you of something that you have seen, read, heard about or experienced before?*
- *If a text title has been given, what does this imply about a possible plot or writing style?*
- *What is the context or topic of the text?*
- *Are there any clues as to when and where the action might take place?*
- *Are there any clues about the environment or setting?*
- *Are any characters mentioned?*
- *What mood does the text create?*
- *Are there any hints as to the aim or purpose of the text?*

Once you have grasped these basic clues, look again at the information in the prompt and think about how you can take it forward or build your writing around it. You may be able to think of different routes that your writing could take. To plot the possible progress of your writing clearly, try noting down your ideas in a quick mind map or flow diagram.

Using this technique to make notes will help you make sure that you fully understand how the mood of the setting and characters is developing. You should also have clearly sketched out some ideas for how the storyline could continue; you can use these to construct your answer.

Once you start writing, it is also a good idea to check that you are following the Key Facts checklist listed on page 18 as they are also relevant for text continuations. However, your writing may have to follow on from a given starting point. If this is the case, you should also try to keep these points in mind.

Top Tip

A paragraph, a sentence or even just a title can give you hints for the plot, characters, scenery and writing style, so use every clue you can find to help build up your writing.

Key Facts

Your writing should:

- continue straight on from where the text finishes, or should include the given phrase or scenario

- develop the given plot line sensibly

- include some or all of the given characters as appropriate

- follow the given text as much as possible in terms of writing style and format: use similar vocabulary terms; construct sentences of a similar style and length; write from the same perspective; and write in the same tense.

www Now it's your turn!

Practise your text continuation writing skills by choosing
one of the question prompts above and completing the
task in your notebook. If you wish to choose prompt 8,
then go to the Bond website and download Appendix 1
Practice activity extracts from the Free Resources section
for this book. Read Extract A and then continue the story.
Think about how your text continuation addresses the
key points raised in this section before asking someone to
comment on your work.

e *Description prompts*

A description prompt is another question type that should be easy for you to identify in
a set of options, as it will usually include a term such as 'describe' (though it may imply
description in a less specific way).

This type of question may provide you with a basis for your description in the form of an
opening paragraph or a visual stimulus and will often give you guidelines on the core points
to include. You may also find that the scope of a prompt is broad enough for you to draw on
either real or imagined experiences as you write your answer. Look at these examples:

includes the term 'describe'

open topic – could be a realistic or imaginary experience

> **9** <u>Describe</u>, in 300 words, how you would spend <u>your perfect day</u>. Consider the
> following points in your answer:
>
> – Where would you be?
>
> – Who would be with you?
>
> – What would you do?   **core points to include**
>
> – Why would it be your perfect day?

implication of description   **specific topic – writing must be realistic and factual**

> **10** <u>Write about</u> your <u>favourite person from history</u>, using no more than 300 words.

As well as forming the focus for specific writing prompts as shown in the examples
above, descriptive passages are often included within other types of writing, such as
fictional narratives. Whether it forms the specific focus or just an element of a piece of
writing, the purpose of descriptive text remains the same; to create a vivid picture that
will not only entertain the reader but will draw them into the text and enable them to
really experience what they are reading.

To ensure that a reader engages with your descriptive writing, try to use a mix of:

- *powerful vocabulary* – stomp *instead of* walk; wail *instead of* cry
- *sense words – what do things* look, sound, feel, taste, smell *like?*
- *adjectives and adverbs – the* blistering *heat; she reappeared* sheepishly
- *similes and metaphors – he was* like a bear with a sore head!*; they awoke slowly, under* the watchful eye of the burning orb.

Including examples of these core elements in your descriptions will bring any piece of descriptive text to life and will help the reader to really experience what you are writing about. (You can read more about these aspects in section B2, 'Develop language skills'.)

 **Key Facts**

When choosing this type of question prompt, also try to remember that descriptive writing:

- is often written as continuous text
- is usually organised in paragraphs
- may be written in the first or third person
- may include direct or reported speech
- can be based on reality or imagination.

 Now it's your turn!

Practise your descriptive writing skills by choosing one of the question prompts above and completing the task in your notebook. Think about how your description addresses the key points raised in this section before asking someone to comment on your work.

 **Top Tip**

You could lose marks for writing too much or too little. Use the number of marks available, word limit guidance and space available to write in, to help you gauge how much to write.

(f) *Visual stimulus prompts*

A visual stimulus prompt is easily identified in a set of options because the question will include a visual aid of some kind, such as a photograph or line drawing. However, the context of this style of question can be quite varied; depending on the scope of the question, you may be provided with some core points to consider.

This style of prompt may require you, for example, to write a piece of fictional or descriptive writing based on the image – giving you an open instruction such as *'Describe what you see'* or *'Write about the image in any way you wish'*. Or, if the image appears as one of a group, you could be asked to write a comparative piece; while if the visual aid is given as part of a text continuation question, then you will need to refer to the image as well as the text in your answer. You could also be asked to use the image as the basis for a debate on a particular topic.

Look at these two examples:

11 Look at this image.

personal opinion implied

Now write <u>a response</u> to the photograph.

Consider the following points in your writing:

• Explore what the image makes you think of.

• Describe how the image makes you feel.

• Explain where and why you think the photograph was taken.

Write no more than 250 words.

core points to include

opening text given

12 '<u>The weather was cold and spitting with rain. He pulled the scarf close around his neck and began walking. A van was parked on the left, facing away from the quayside. He knew exactly what to do ...</u>'

Using this opening paragraph and the photograph as your starting point, write a piece of <u>creative writing</u>. Write no more than 350 words.

implies fictional narrative

You may feel that choosing a question that includes a visual stimulus is a safe option because you will have been given a clear image to focus all or part of your answer around. However, you need to be sure that you have understood the context of the question – which style of writing the visual stimulus is being used in – and that you are comfortable writing in this style. While the visual stimulus should be a useful starting point, there are still several questions that you need to ask yourself before you write. For example:

- *Are you clear about how the question prompt is using the visual aid? – are you being asked to describe the image and your reaction to it or to use it as a springboard for a fictional narrative, factual piece, debate, etc? Do you feel confident writing in this style?*
- *Is the image clear? – can you work out what the subject of the image is? Is it showing people, animals, buildings or a landscape, for example?*
- *Can you easily form an opinion about what the image is showing? – what does it make you think of or feel? Does it remind you of anything that you may have seen before?*
- *Can you pick out any clues from the image that you can use in your writing? – can you spot anything unusual that you could draw on?*
- *Is the image accompanied by any additional information, such as core points to consider? – how easy do you think it will be to incorporate these points into your writing?*

Remember, the aim and purpose of the question prompt will determine how you use the visual aid, what you write and how you write it.

www   Now it's your turn!

Practise your visual stimulus writing skills by choosing one of the question prompts above and completing the task in your notebook. Think about how your writing addresses the key points raised in this section before asking someone to comment on your work.

! Top Tip

As we have seen here, some question prompts will combine more than one question type. Make sure that you read a question closely to work out which formats and styles an examiner will be looking for in your answer.

(g) Playscript prompts

Playscript prompts should be quite simple to identify within a set of options because they will usually include the terms 'play', 'script', 'playscript' or possibly 'scene'. For this question type you might expect to be given a scenario outline that you have to develop in script form, or you may have the opening extract from a script that you then have to continue. Here are two example question prompts:

includes the term 'playscript'   **scenario outline given**

13   Develop the following scenario in the form of a <u>playscript</u>. '<u>Sophie is trying to persuade her mum to let her go round to her friend's house after school tomorrow</u>.' Write no more than two sides of A4 paper.

14 <u>Continue</u> this <u>scene</u>. Write up to two sides of A4 paper.

Dad: Is that the post?

Philip: Yes – there's just one letter for me and a telephone bill.

Dad: A letter for you? You don't usually get letters.

> **opening text given**

[*Philip opens the letter and begins to read it aloud*]

Philip: Dear Philip, Congratulations! You have won first place in the competition ...

Playscripts can seem quite straightforward to write as the plot and development of each character is seen largely through direct speech and action rather than continuous narrative. However, if you choose this type of question prompt you need to remember that scripts follow a very different style and structure to other forms of writing.

As you write your playscript extract, try to ask yourself several key questions such as:

- *What type of play is it? – a monologue, a farce, a tragedy? Different types of plays are likely to need different features and dialogue styles.*
- *Which section of the play are you writing? – think about the plot details you have been given, what may have happened previously and what may happen after your scene.*
- *How many characters do you need? – look at how many are introduced in the question prompt. Do you need to include them all? Are any new characters needed? Remember, though, if you bring in too many the plot line could become confusing.*
- *Do you need a narrator? – an outside observer can provide commentary on the action, links between events, and a conclusion.*
- *What style of dialogue should you use? – if you are continuing a scene then your dialogue should follow the same style as the given text, so check whether it has been written in Standard English, colloquial (slang) terms or a particular dialect.*

 **Key Facts**

Also, try to remember that plays:

- are usually divided into Acts, with each act divided into Scenes
- display character names clearly on the left hand side of the page and are separated from each section of their dialogue by a colon
- indicate that a new character is speaking by starting their dialogue on a new line
- include notes (stage directions) on scenery, props, lighting and sound effects and characters' appearances, actions and movements; these create atmosphere and are written in brackets.

Speech marks are not used in playscripts.

www Now it's your turn!

Practise your script writing skills by choosing one of the question prompts above and completing the task in your notebook. Think about how your playscript addresses the key points raised in this section before asking someone to comment on your work.

For more guidance on how playscripts should be written, why not read *Bond How to do ...11⁺ English*, section C7 and *The secrets of Comprehension*, section B1: 'Recognise different text types'. (See the Additional resources appendix in section C (online) for details.)

(h) *Given text prompts*

We have already seen some examples of prompts where you could be given a section of text to refer to in your answer (different forms of text continuations, for example). We have also seen that the amount of text given could range from just a few lines to a much longer extract. However, a prompt that includes a given text may not always require you to write a text continuation. Look at these two examples:

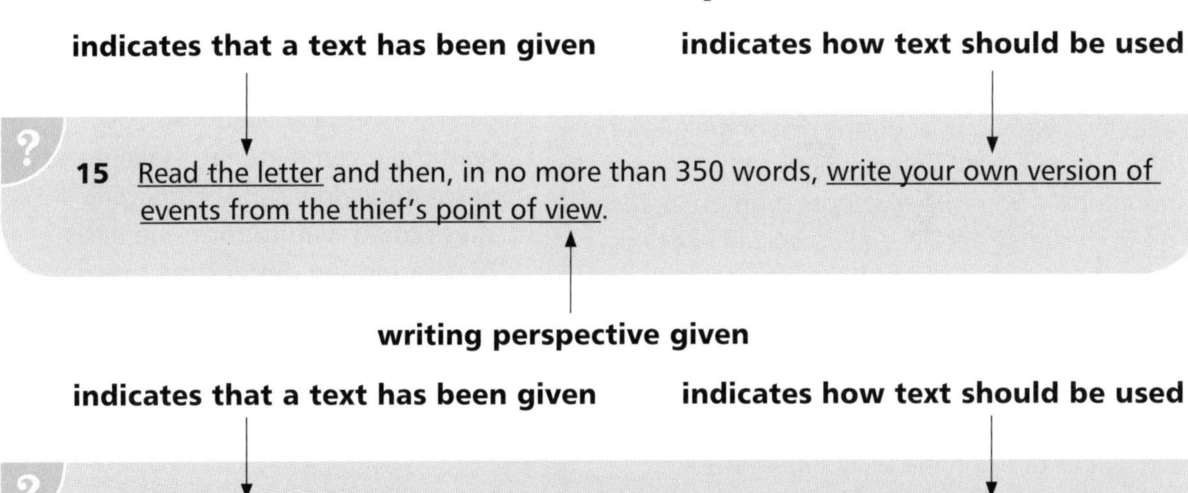

You may feel that choosing this style of question is a wise option because you already have a given piece of text to use for reference and that forms a starting point for your own ideas. However, in the same way as for prompts that include visual aids, you must be sure that you understand how this type of prompt is using the given text. The context for this style of prompt can be quite varied, so try to ask yourself some key questions before you write, such as:

- *Are you clear about how the question prompt is using the text? – are you being asked to use the given information to write about an event from a different viewpoint? Or perhaps to rewrite (convert) the content of the text into a different format (from a factual report into a story; a playscript into a letter; a diary entry into a report, etc.)? Do you feel confident writing in this style?*
- *Is it clear how much freedom you will have in your writing? – do you need to stay close to the content of the given text or does the prompt allow you to use your imagination?*
- *Can you pick out any clues from the text that you can use in your writing? – look for direct and implied details of characters, scenery, locations and plot lines.*
- *Do you need to consider the style of language that has been used in the given text? – will you need to follow this style and tone in your writing?*
- *Do you need to form an opinion about the given text style or topic before you write? – how easy is this to do? What does it make you think of or feel? Does it remind you of anything you may have seen before?*

Being clear about the context of the question, and the writing style it requires, will help you to ensure that the aim and purpose of your writing will be appropriate for the task. Remember to keep the question prompt in your mind at all times, as this will help you to write a focused answer.

www Now it's your turn!

Practise using a given text as a springboard for your own writing by choosing one of the question prompts above and completing the task in your notebook. If you wish to choose prompt 15, then go to the Bond website and download Appendix 1 Practice activity extracts from the Free Resources section for this book. Read Extract B before writing your answer. If you wish to answer prompt 16, then first read Extract C from the online appendix. Think about how your writing addresses the key points raised in this section before asking someone to comment on your work.

! Top Tip

Underlining key pieces of information can be especially useful. As you read the given material, make notes or jot down ideas in the margin – these could help to form the basis of your writing. For further tips on reading for clues see *The secrets of Comprehension*, section B1 'Read and understand the text' pages 7–26.

(i) Report and recount prompts

Report and recount prompts are common question types that are usually easy to spot amongst a set of options by the use of the terms 'report' or 'recount', though these specific terms may not always be included. Guidelines on the core points you should consider in your answer are also often provided. Here are two examples:

17 Write a <u>report</u> entitled: '<u>Tourism and my region</u>'.

You may like to consider the following questions:

– Where is the region and how can someone get there?

– What is the history of the area?

– What is the climate like?

– What is there to see and do?

– Where can someone eat? drink? sleep?

– When is the best/worst time to visit?

– Where can someone get more information?

Your report should be no more than two sides of A4 paper.

18 You witnessed a traffic accident this morning while out walking your dog.

A car hit a tree after driving too quickly around a corner.

As you approached the crash site, the driver and passenger were getting out.

The police have now asked you to write a <u>personal statement explaining what you saw</u>. Limit your statement to 250 words.

Reports and recounts share many of the same features and characteristics: they can both be fictional or factual and may focus on a wide range of topics or themes; they can both include diagrams or images; they are usually written in continuous text and both follow an organised structure. What is more, the purpose of a report will determine its style and this means that some reports may actually be closer to recounts than non-chronological report writing!

If you find it difficult sometimes to work out which style you should be writing in, try to remember that, generally:

- *recount writing is used for texts such as biographies, diaries, personal accounts of visits or events and subjective newspaper and magazine articles*
- *report writing is used for texts such as writing up experiments or school projects, weather forecasts, advice leaflets and objective newspaper and magazine articles.*

As you write, you may also find it helpful to try and recall the following checklist that highlights the fundamental differences between reports and recounts:

	Report	Recount
Aim	to inform the reader	to inform and often entertain the reader
Purpose	to categorise and record information clearly	to retell an event or activity as the writer believes, or wishes the reader to believe, it occurred
Writing style	impersonal – usually written in third person (*he, she, people, the Romans ...*); formal language	personal – usually written in first person (*I, we, our ...*); formal or informal language
Writing tone	factual; includes subject-specific or technical vocabulary if needed	often emotional and descriptive; includes subject-specific or technical vocabulary if needed
Writing tense	usually present tense (except for historical reports)	usually past tense
Writing focus	discusses general aspects and facts	discusses specific people and/or events
Structure: *introduction*	general opening statement or paragraph to introduce topic	first paragraph sets the scene (*who, when, where, what ...*)
Structure: *main content*	details organised in non-chronological order; similar ideas and themes grouped in paragraphs and often arranged under section headings	details organised in chronological order; series of events separated into paragraphs and linked by time connectives (*first, then, next, finally ...*)
Structure: *final paragraph*	draws report to appropriate conclusion	draws recount to a close, may offer a summary and/or evaluation of events

www Now it's your turn!

Practise your report and recount writing skills by choosing one of the question prompts above and completing the task in your notebook. Think about how your report or recount addresses the key points raised in this section before asking someone to comment on your work.

Top Tip

For examples of reports, you might like to:

- read your school report or the weather forecasts in the newspaper
- look at a wide variety of leaflets showing you how to make the most of your local library, for example, or pick them up in the doctor's, dentist's or vet's waiting room.

(j) Review prompts

You can usually identify a review prompt quite easily in a set of options, as it often includes the term 'review' or a phrase implying that an individual response is required. Additionally, this type of writing prompt often focuses on aspects of literature. For example, a question might relate to a specific character or a memorable episode, or it could refer more generally to a familiar book, play, poem, film or writer.

Reviews are a type of report writing but, as they rely on the writer giving their own critical assessment of something, they also share similarities with recount writing. Review prompts offer you the chance to explore your own thoughts, feelings and opinions and to show your personal preferences. However, you may not always be given guidance on the core points to include in your response.

Let's look at two examples:

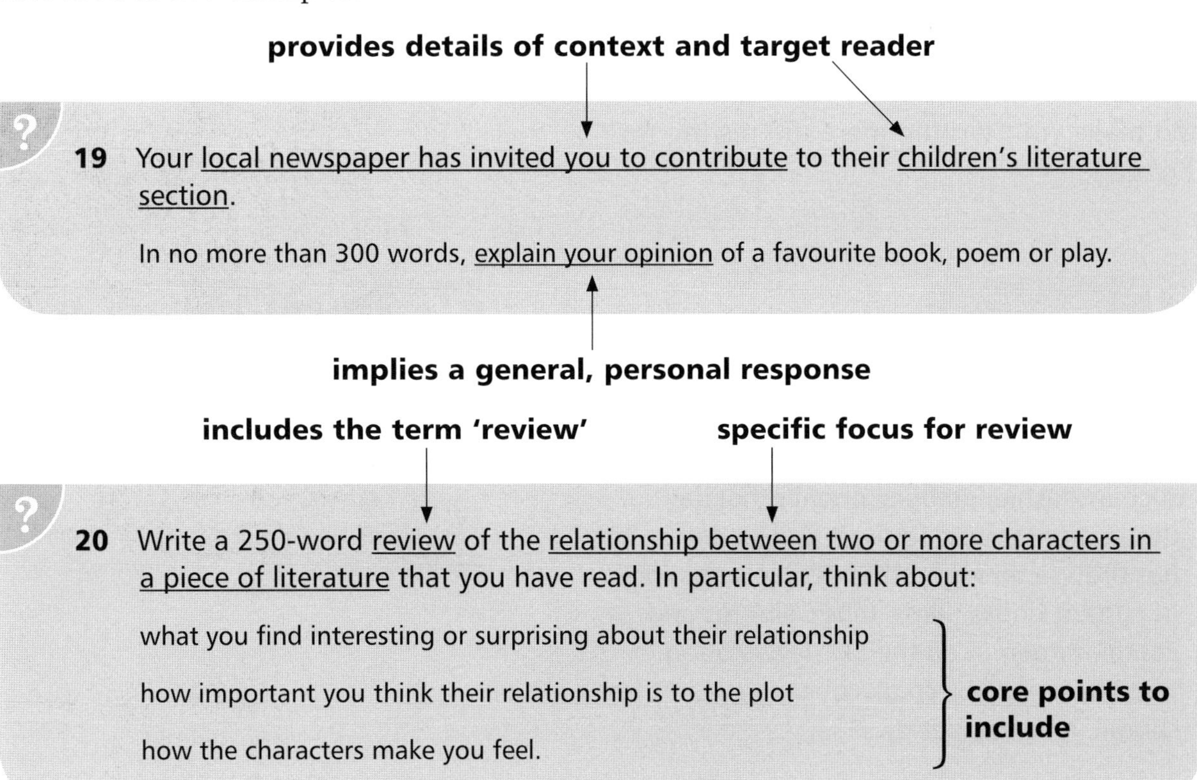

Whether you are focusing on an aspect of literature (a character, book, play, film, poem, or particular writer, for example), or on something more general (such as a computer game, restaurant or holiday resort), your review should:

- be written in the first or third person – '*I felt that* …'; '*this game* is designed for …'

- follow a logical, organised structure – try to write in themed paragraphs, which you might choose to arrange under section headings

- set the scene – so for a book, include brief details of author, title, plot, writing style and target audience, for example

- be relevant for your reader – think about who the review is for and what they will be most interested to know; but make sure that you don't give the ending away if you are writing about a piece of fiction!

- present a balanced view – include some highlights (strengths) and lowlights (weaknesses)

- offer a conclusion – this could be a summary of your opinion or a recommendation to your reader, for example.

Recalling your own thoughts about something can often be a challenge under timed conditions. However, you should find it much easier if you can develop a broad bank of ideas to draw on. To create this bank, try to make a note of any positive or negative thoughts, feelings or reactions you have while you read or watch something or after you have visited somewhere. If you can include some of these strong feelings in a review, they will help to inject some passion and emotion into your response and make your writing more interesting for the reader.

Top Tip

Try using a highlighter pen to emphasise your notes about any strong views and opinions you have had. This should help you to recall your thoughts afterwards.

Top Tip

Look out for reviews in magazines or newspapers. They might cover a wide range of interesting products, services and events such as: fashion, mobile phones, holiday destinations, music festivals and so on. Or why not browse through other people's opinions of current books, films, music albums and computer games on the BBC Newsround website (news.bbc.co.uk/cbbcnews) and then submit your own reviews?

Parent Tip

Try to give your child as many opportunities as possible to read reviews as this will help to familiarise them with this style of writing. The weekend newspapers are especially good for reviews of films, programmes, music and places to visit.

(k) Debate prompts

These question prompts are normally quite easy to recognise as they often present a discussion topic in the form of a question or a statement and then invite you to respond to it. Look out for key terms such as 'explain', 'discuss', 'argue' and 'consider' – these all imply that you will need to debate one or more issues and include your own opinion in your answer. Here are two examples:

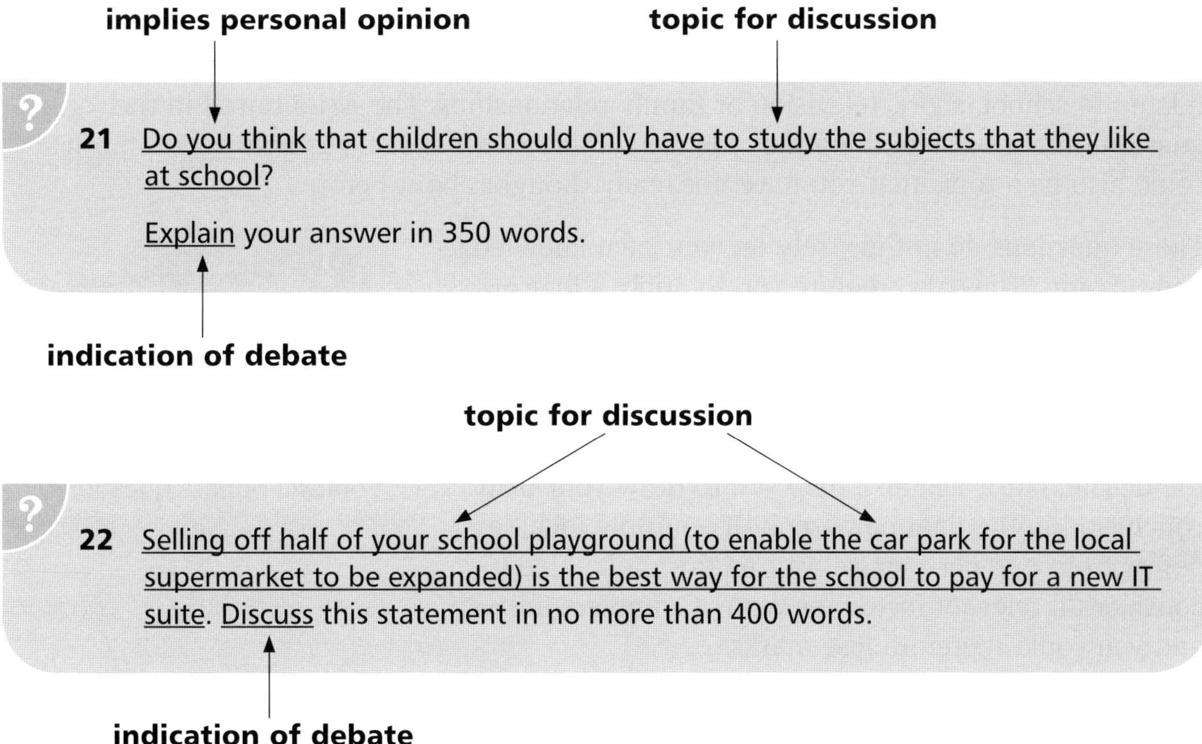

You may feel that debating questions are one of the hardest forms of writing task because they require you to evaluate a range of views about an issue and then draw your own conclusion, based on the facts that you have presented. Don't worry; many children (and adults!) find these question types difficult.

Before you think about the specific topic that a debate prompt raises, try to remember that your answer should:

- include relevant facts as well as your own opinion
- refer to any given text in addition to your own knowledge where useful
- discuss positive and negative elements of the issue or argument clearly
- explain each point concisely
- avoid repetition of the same points
- use persuasive language
- follow a clear structure, using paragraphs to organise ideas
- draw to a clear conclusion.

Debate questions can be based on a wide variety of themes or topics, which makes them hard to prepare for. For example, a question may relate to a theme in a given comprehension text or other piece of literature, a recent topic in the news or an issue related to school, sport, television or family relationships. The issue raised in the question might be something that you are familiar with or feel strongly about, but it could also be a topic that you have not really thought about before.

These questions do not just rely on your own knowledge and opinion. They also require you to apply a logical thought process so that you can 'dissect' the issue and put together some realistic viewpoints. Your answer should also present a balanced argument. This will not only provide the reader with a considered overview of the debate, but it will also help you to draw your own conclusion in the final paragraph. If you only include points from one perspective, you might not be able to consider all relevant factors or write a complete answer and you could therefore lose marks.

See section B2 'Create a plan' (page 51) for a useful 4-point strategy that can help you to tackle debate questions.

Newspaper and magazine articles, as well as television and radio interviews, documentaries and phone-in programmes, are often based around debates. Try listening to or reading a debate and then writing down the various points that are made in the discussion. If you divide your page in half, you can easily jot down points that are both for and against the issue. Then, at the bottom of the page, make a note of any conclusions drawn or summary that is given. (You will find that sometimes no clear resolution will be reached!) When you have made your notes, ask yourself what your personal view of the topic is and why – also think about what has persuaded you to come to this conclusion.

 Now it's your turn!

Practise your debate writing skills by choosing one of the prompts above and completing the task in your notebook. Think about how your debate addresses the key points raised in this section before asking someone to comment on your work.

Encourage your child to form debates that argue for or against a given view. This can be particularly beneficial with children who have more argumentative natures because it can be an excellent way of channelling their energy. Stopping to consider both points of view should also help to take away any competitive need that they might feel to win an argument.

● Adopt the right style

Whatever the focus of a writing task might be, you should always try to think about the aim and purpose of the piece of writing. Who are you writing for and why? The aim of the writing and the expected reader are important factors in determining the style or styles that you need to apply. This section provides some useful checklists and reminders that should help you to choose the appropriate style for any writing task.

Now that you know how to recognise different types of writing prompt, read your chosen task(s) carefully and first think about whether the aim of your writing should be to:

- **inform:** *informative writing provides the information that the reader needs, wants or ought to know in a clear and organised way. Facts are delivered without any bias or slant from the writer, creating a balanced, fair and trustworthy account.*

- **explain:** *explanatory writing outlines the facts and then shows the reader why the topic or issue is important to them (or to the writer). The writer's perspective may either be objective or subjective, but the information provided should be clear, balanced and factual.*

- **describe:** *descriptive writing often uses different layers of detail to outline a scene, event or person. To be successful it must appeal to a reader's senses in order to create mood and atmosphere. Its aim is to fully engage the reader's imagination and enable them to really experience what is being described, not just read about it.*

- **argue:** *effective argumentative writing shows the reader a well-considered point of view and supports it with evidence. It is likely to consider other valid arguments and will then try to counter or respond to them with logical and careful thought. The aim of this writing style is to present a balanced view of a topic or issue and for the writer ultimately to show the reader why their opinion is more well-founded and rational than other viewpoints.*

- **persuade:** *persuasive writing also aims to influence the reader's opinion but the writer's point of view comes across much more strongly. The tone is more passionate, emotional and personal, so the debate is much more one-sided (biased). Including techniques such as similes, metaphors and short sentences for maximum effect, the writer's main aim is to convince the reader that the view they have put forward is the right one.*

- **advise:** *advice writing adopts a soft (more subtle) approach in order to explain something. Using terms such as 'should', 'could' and 'might', it provides helpful and*

Next, think carefully about who you are writing for because different types of reader will probably require different styles of writing.

Does the context of the question imply that you are writing to a town councillor, a friend, a group of young children, the general public or the examiner, for example? This is important because the way you might structure a letter to a town councillor would be different to how you might write to a close friend. The level of vocabulary and sentence structure that would be appropriate for a review in a children's magazine would differ from a report written just for the examiner, and so on.

Different readers may also have certain expectations about your writing, based on some standard rules of written English. For instance, a reader should easily be able to recognise a letter, poem or playscript by the layout of the text on the page. However, if, for example, you wrote a playscript without putting the characters' names on the left hand side of the page, the reader could become confused and not understand that the text should be read as a script. This, in turn, would mean that your plot line and characters could be difficult to identify and that the reading flow of your writing would seem disjointed. Try to remember that the layout of a text can help to give the reader clues as to how they should approach a piece of writing, as well as to the content. It is therefore important to keep aspects of standard layouts in mind when you are choosing your question prompt and preparing your writing.

Thinking about your reader while you are writing any type of text will help to make sure that your vocabulary, content, writing style and layout are all suited to the task.

A reader should feel satisfied after they have read something, so try to think about what particular readers might expect. For example, imagine a young child's reaction if they heard a story where all of the characters were harmed or died at the end; or a police officer's response to a formal complaint letter that was full of jokes. Recognising different forms of writing, and the type of reader that you are writing for, can help you to understand what is appropriate for different readers.

Finally, when thinking about your writing style, you might also find it helpful to ask yourself some questions such as:

- *Should I write in Standard or non-Standard English?*
- *Should I write in the first, second or third person?*
- *Should my vocabulary be simple or complex?*
- *Should the tone of my writing be:*
  - *formal or informal?*
  - *objective or subjective?*
  - *functional or imaginative?*
  - *literal (direct) or figurative (descriptive)?*

See the checklists below for some quick reminders of the main features for these eight writing styles and examples of when you might use them.

a Formal v. informal writing

Formal	Informal
coherent – clear structure and direction	haphazard – may lack direction in parts
concise – no waffle or extra detail	rambling – may occasionally drift away from the core focus
professional, unbiased tone – uses first person sparingly	chatty, relaxed tone – over-use of first person creates a very personal, familiar style; potential to add bias
precise terms – avoids vague or general descriptions, e.g. 'nice', 'good', 'things'	casual approach to language – can include poor grammar
careful punctuation – e.g. uses exclamation marks and brackets sparingly	more casual punctuation – includes exclamation marks, dashes, etc. for emphasis
uses Standard English – avoids contractions, colloquialisms and slang	may reflect regional dialects and 'everyday speech' – including contractions, colloquialisms and slang
can include lengthy and complex sentence structures	more simple sentence structures
appropriate for tasks that, for example, involve writing: reports, official letters, debates, explanatory text, instructions and newspaper articles	appropriate for tasks that, for example, involve writing: narrative, personal letters, diary entries and magazine articles

www Now it's your turn!

Download Appendix 1 Practice activity extracts from the Free Resources section for this book from our website. Read and compare the examples of formal and informal writing shown in Extracts D and E. Then write one formal letter to your Headteacher and one informal letter to your penfriend regarding the prize that you have won in the school raffle.

(b) Objective v. subjective writing

Objective	Subjective
impersonal style – avoids use of first person (I, you, we)	personal style – first person often used
avoids emotive language – aim is to inform, not persuade	emotive language – aim is to influence, not just inform
adopts neutral approach to information, facts, details about the topic or theme	provides information, facts and so on but with biased perspective
detached, impartial writing – no information about the writer; often uses passive voice	refers directly to the author, tells us how the writer thinks and feels
often uses formal language	often uses informal language
appropriate for tasks that, for example, involve writing: reports, explanatory text, instructions and advice	appropriate for tasks that, for example, involve writing: personal comment (e.g. reviews, recounts, newspaper articles) and persuasive text (e.g. debates, advertising slogans)

www Now it's your turn!

Download Appendix 1 Practice activity extracts from the Free Resources section for this book from our website. Read and compare the examples of objective and subjective writing shown in Extracts F and G. Then write one objective paragraph and one subjective paragraph about the village, town or city that you live in.

(c) Functional v. imaginative writing

Functional	Imaginative
content often factual	content often fictional
aim is to explain, describe or analyse topic; to inform the reader	aim is to help reader imagine and explore topic; to entertain the reader
straightforward, neutral language – words mean exactly what they say	emotive and descriptive language – uses imagery, e.g. similes, metaphors, alliteration, personification
appropriate for tasks that, for example, involve writing: notes, instructions, reports, news articles, explanatory text (e.g. extracts from a textbook)	appropriate for tasks that, for example, involve writing: letters, diary entries, playscripts, stories, poems, reviews and recounts

www Now it's your turn!

Download Appendix 1 Practice activity extracts from the Free Resources section for this book from our website. Read and compare the examples of functional and imaginative writing shown in Extracts H and I. Then write a functional and an imaginative account based on the same event that happened on a memorable day in school. You might like to try writing a poem for your imaginative piece, but remember that you can use several writing styles for a piece of imaginative writing – see the table above for more ideas.

(d) Literal v. figurative writing

Literal	Figurative
words convey meaning directly to reader	words create pictures in reader's mind which convey meaning more vividly
straightforward writing; describes something exactly as it is	imaginative writing; adds colour and interest to writing – boosts description
includes simple words and descriptions	includes descriptive techniques such as similes, metaphors, personification and hyperbole
appropriate for tasks that, for example, involve writing: formal and informal letters, explanatory texts, instructions, reports, newspaper and magazine articles, narrative, playscripts, reviews and recounts	appropriate for tasks that, for example, involve writing: descriptions, stories, poems, songs, recounts, reviews and informal letters

Now it's your turn!

Download Appendix 1 Practice activity extracts from the Free Resources section for this book from our website. Read and compare the examples of literal and figurative writing shown in Extracts J and K. Then write about your favourite game (board game, computer game or sports game) in both a literal and a figurative style.

! Top Tip

When you next pick up something to read (a book, letter, comic, review, poem, magazine or newspaper article, for example) see how many different writing styles and literary features you can recognise.

✓ Parent Tip

Often a child will need to combine two or more writing styles to ensure that a piece of writing meets the requirements of a task. To help your child understand how different writing styles can be used together, encourage them to look out for a range of styles as they read or draw attention to them as you read together. The wider a child reads, the more styles they are likely to come across. As they do so, they should also gradually become more familiar with the literary features and techniques that each style uses and should start to feel more confident about using them in their own writing.

2 Improve your writing

● Generate creative ideas

You may often find that thinking of an original idea or ideas is more difficult than the actual writing stage. If so, don't panic! This is a common problem for many adults and children alike; particularly in timed or exam conditions. This section explores three practical techniques that should prove useful the next time you get stuck for ideas, whether you are in an exam or writing in a more relaxed environment.

(a) Search your memory

Our memories can be a great source of ideas that can be used in different ways to form the basis for many types of factual or creative writing. For example, a memory can be a sound starting point for a response to a letter or debate prompt, or it can make the perfect foundation for a poem or story.

Whatever the style of writing prompt, it is often easier to start from what you know. So, look at the theme or context of a question and then try tapping into related memories of your own experiences. To give you a sense of how this technique might work, the table below shows a range of possible themes that a writing prompt could refer to and some potential memories that these themes might bring to mind.

Writing theme	Memories that a writing prompt might trigger
Families	• Having a new brother or sister. • Visiting your grandparents.
Friendships	• When you first met your best friend. • Sleepovers at a friend's house.
Heroes and Heroines	• Your favourite heroic character from a book, programme or film. • Picking a role model (e.g. a family member, or a TV, film or sports personality).
School	• Your first day at school. • Taking part in an assembly or school concert.
Holidays	• The best or worst holiday you have had. • Your first camping or caravanning trip.
Celebrations	• Christmas, birthdays, Halloween, Guy Fawkes Night, Easter, Diwali, Eid-Ul-Fitr, Jamshedi Noruz, Losar, Naw-Ruz, or Rosh Hashannah. • Making the food and decorating the house ready for a party.
Hobbies	• Playing a musical instrument for a concert or singing in a choir. • Joining the cubs, scouts, rainbows, brownies, guides or other group.
Health	• Going into hospital to have an operation. • The first time you lost a tooth.
Animals and birds	• Making a feeder for the birds in your garden. • Going to a farm, zoo, nature reserve or safari park.
The environment and nature	• Helping to grow plants or vegetables in the garden or allotment. • Climbing a mountain or going for a long walk.

If a writing prompt does trigger one or more of your memories, try to ask yourself some key questions about each one. For example:

- *What happened? Where did it happen and when?*
- *Who was involved?*
- *How did I feel at the time?*
- *How do I feel looking back on the event?*
- *What have I learnt from the experience?*
- *Why is this such a strong memory?*

Thinking about questions like these will help you to get the most out of your memories, giving you as much detail as possible to use as a base for your writing. Let's have a look at how this might work with the following writing prompt:

1 In no more than 300 words, recount an occasion when you felt proud of yourself.

This prompt might bring to mind several occasions, such as a time when you performed a solo in a school concert. If you then ask yourself some key questions about this memory your notes might look something like this:

Topic: personal achievement	Triggered memory: solo performance in school concert.
What happened? Where? When?	*End-of-year concert; I played the flute.*
Who was involved?	*All of Year 6 performed in either music, drama or dance. Parents and families watched.*
How did I feel at the time?	*Nervous – the hall was full of people; didn't want to make a mistake. Afterwards, felt like a star – was told I played well.*
How do I feel looking back on it?	*Proud of myself; much braver.*
What have I learnt from the experience?	*I enjoy performing and playing the flute. Joined the school orchestra and want to join the jazz band.*
Why is it such a strong memory?	*The first time that I was under pressure; showed me I could cope when performing in front of people.*

Having noted down the key points of your memory, you could then use them to structure your writing as follows:

Every Year 6 pupil took part in the end-of-year school concert. Some of my friends were in a play, others played musical instruments and some performed a dance routine. I chose to play the flute.

I was so nervous. I wasn't sure whether I would be able to cope with the pressure or whether my hands would stop shaking! I was called on stage straight after the interval and could not believe how many people were in the audience. They were all looking at me. I felt a little sick as I turned to my music and brought the flute up to my lips. Trying hard to look only at the music, I took a deep breath and began.

Surprisingly, I think I played better than ever before. When I had finished, the audience started clapping loudly and some people were cheering. I could see my mum and dad and they looked so pleased that I thought they would burst! After the concert was over, three teachers came over to me to say how well they thought I had played and my friends' parents also said that they enjoyed my solo. I felt like a famous musician and I didn't want the evening to end. Although I had been nervous to start with, I felt very proud of myself afterwards.

I have played the flute much more since. In September, I auditioned for my secondary school orchestra and got accepted. I am also thinking of joining the youth jazz band in my town so that I can get more practice. I would never have thought that my school concert would have been so important to me but it showed me that I can cope under pressure. It started a real love for music, for playing the flute and for performing.

Of course, there is no rule that says you have to write an exact version of something that really happened. You can create some wonderful fictional narratives, for example, by using your own memories as a base or springboard and then adding to or altering the actual events as much as you want to fit the task. Following this technique will help your writing sound more realistic because it will have been built around a real memory, but it will also allow you to be really creative.

Read the following fictional narrative prompt:

2 Write about the following title in any way you wish: The day it all began. Write up to one side of A4 paper.

The theme of this title is very broad so you could probably tap into many different memories to help you structure your writing. This prompt might, for instance, bring to mind the same school concert memory. If so, you might use your notes of this memory to develop the following piece of fictional narrative:

The advert had been splashed across the local newspapers urging anyone with a talent to come forward. The winner of the regional heat would go on to compete in the live television programme for a chance to be named the best talent in the country. I was surprised when I won the first round of local auditions and then even more shocked when I won the second one. Suddenly there I was, facing the final stage of auditions in my area. Whoever the judges picked as the winner would appear live on television next Saturday evening. This was it. A man with a clipboard smiled at me and urged me on to the stage.

I had chosen to play a solo on my flute and I was so nervous. I wasn't sure whether I would be able to cope with the pressure or whether my hands would stop shaking long enough for me to even pick up the instrument! I looked at the three judges sat in a row in front of me. I had their full attention. I felt a little sick as I brought the flute up to my lips. Trying hard to look only at the music, I took a deep breath and began. Surprisingly, I think I played better than ever before. When I had finished the judges smiled, thanked me for my performance, and asked me to go back and wait in the reception area.

Once all of the final auditions were over we were all called back on to the stage and the judges stood up ready to tell us the result. A journalist from the local newspaper was there to interview the winner and take their photo and a television crew were also ready to capture the exciting moment. The head judge began by thanking everyone for taking part and then, after a long pause, he called out my name as the winner! I stood still, blinking in shock as it gradually sunk in that he had said my name. I heard lots of cheering and clapping; suddenly, I felt like a celebrity and I didn't want the evening to end.

Saturday night has come around quickly and now here I am about to perform for millions of television viewers as well as the studio audience. I hope to be in the competition for as long as possible; it would be a dream come true to be named 'the best talent in the country'. How many weeks I survive on stage is down to the viewers, so if you are watching and you enjoy my performance, please vote for me! I would never have thought that a small, local audition would have been so important to me, but it certainly showed me that I am able to cope under pressure. It has also started a real love for music, for playing the flute and for performing.

Compare the piece of narrative above to the first recount. Can you recognise which elements of the real memory have been used to form the foundations (basic structure) for this piece of writing?

You may find that one memory can act as the base for several different types of writing prompts. Let's see how this might work for the following examples of a typical debate prompt (3), description prompt (4), fictional narrative prompt (5) and review prompt (6).

3 Discuss the following question: Should wild animals be kept in captivity? Write up to one side of A4 paper.

4 In no more than 350 words, describe how you would spend your perfect day. Consider the following points in your answer:

– Where would you be? – Who would be with you?

– What would you do? – Why would it be your perfect day?

5 A day in the life of a gorilla. Write up to one side of A4 paper.

6 You have been asked to submit an article for your local magazine's weekly feature: 'Something for the weekend'. Your brief is to write a 300-word review of one activity, event or place that would be appropriate for a family day out.

At first glance you might find it difficult to think of one memory that could be drawn on for any of the four prompts given above. Did the topic of the first prompt bring anything to mind? Perhaps a visit you have made to a zoo, as this type of place is not a natural environment for wild animals?

Through asking yourself some key questions about a memory like this, you might make similar notes to the examples given in the diagram on page 43.

You should be able to see that asking yourself these types of questions could help to give you some points to think about and include in a response to the debate question (3) above.

But you could also use the same memory as a basis for prompt four. Look back at the description prompt and think about it in relation to the idea of a zoo visit. Perhaps the perfect day you could describe would be the opportunity of being a keeper at the zoo for a day, drawing on what you remember the keepers doing and on what you learned about the animals during your visit.

What about prompt five? An ideal springboard for this piece of fictional narrative could be the gorillas you saw at the zoo (their enclosure, their food, their actions and behaviour and so on) or perhaps what you learned about gorillas in the wild. You could then use this knowledge to help put yourself in the animal's place and examine one day at the zoo or out in the natural habitat from the gorilla's perspective.

And for prompt six? The memory of your visit should provide plenty of detail for a review of what a zoo has to offer as a family day out. For example, you might recall the range of animals that are at the zoo and the most interesting animals to see; any

What happened? Where? When?
- School trip to London Zoo in Easter holiday.
- Saw different exhibits and enclosures for: tropical birds, butterflies, gorillas, vultures, camels, lions, tigers, hippos, penguins, zebras, giraffes.
- Keepers talked to us about the animals; we watched the gorillas and monkeys being fed.
- Touched a snake; a butterfly landed on my head.
- Filled in worksheets, looked at animal bones, and watched a video about the rainforest.
- Lots of other school trips and families were there.

What have I learnt from the experience?
- Animals take a lot of time, money and research to look after; wild animals should not be kept as pets.
- Different animals need different habitats, diets, etc.
- Some zoos used to display animals for public pleasure without thinking much about animal welfare.
- Some animals in zoos are now extinct in the wild.
- Zoos help to educate people about animals.
- Zoos run breeding programmes and conservation projects.

Topic: Animals in captivity

Triggered memory: Visiting London Zoo

Who was involved?
- 20 pupils
- 2 teachers
- Zoo keepers

How do I feel looking back on it?
- Good day out, would like to go again.
- Would like to be a keeper for a day.
- The animals were well looked after by trained keepers.
- Some of the enclosures seemed a bit cramped.
- Do animals mind being stared at by so many people?
- Should animals be in their own natural habitats?

How did I feel at the time?
- Excited on the coach.
- Lions and tigers were a bit scary.
- Gorillas and monkeys were fascinating.
- Fishy air around penguin area made me feel sick.
- Tired on the way home.

special daily events such as 'meet the animal sessions' or animal feeding times; the types of facts that children and adults can learn about the different animals; where you can get something to eat and drink; where the zoo is and how much it costs to get in; its opening times and the best time to go to beat the crowds; why you think it's a good place to go for all the family and so on.

Top Tip

To help you prompt and structure your memories, think about attaching six key words to each hand like this:

Can you see how you might be able to draw a lot of ideas for different types of writing from just one memory? Using your own experiences as a springboard for writing can help to save time in your planning stages as well as make your writing feel more realistic.

Now it's your turn!

First, read each of the questions below.

1 You slept soundly last night in your own bed but on waking this morning you have found that you are in an unfamiliar room. You also realise that you don't quite feel like yourself. You walk over to the mirror and are shocked to see someone else staring back at you. Recount the events of your day as either a diary entry or a playscript. Write up to two sides of A4 paper.

2 Discuss the following statement in no more than 400 words: Playing games should be restricted to weekends and holiday periods.

3 You have been asked to submit an article for your local magazine's weekly entertainment feature. Your brief is to write a 350-word review of one form of entertainment that you feel would be of interest to children aged 10–11 years.

4 In 350 words, describe how you would spend your ideal afternoon. You may find it helpful to think about some of the following questions in your answer:
  – What type of activity would you do?   – How many people would be involved?
  – What equipment would you need?   – Where would you be?
  – Would it cost anything?   – Who else might enjoy spending time in the same way?

Now, try to think of **one** memory that you could use as a basis for an answer to any of the four question prompts. Next, choose one prompt and ask yourself some of the key questions that we have looked at in this section and note down your thoughts about your memory. Then, write three brief outlines that show how you could use this memory and your notes about it as a starting point for each of the other writing prompts. Finally, discuss your notes about each prompt with someone and explain how your one memory has sparked off ideas for all four questions.

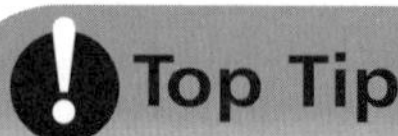

Top Tip

If you're not sure where to start, look at the second prompt. It talks about 'playing games' but it doesn't specify what type of games. Could this help you to recall a memory about playing a computer game, a board game, a card game, a character role-play game or a team game at school, for example? How could you use a memory like this as a starting point for each of the other prompts?

b Interrogate and interview

This may sound like a 'scary' section, but this technique is a really useful way of creating details and for generating ideas. Interviews are something that we are all likely to experience at some point, for example: you may have an interview before you start at secondary school, or if you want to join a higher education college or a university in a few years, or for any job that you apply for.

Top Tip

Try this technique whenever you suffer from 'writer's block'. It can be a quick and easy way of getting your ideas flowing!

The aim of an interview is to 'examine or interrogate by questioning' in order to find out the facts and details about someone or something. Some job roles such as a journalist, a police officer, a researcher, a radio or television presenter and a psychologist involve interviewing people regularly. However, this investigative approach can also be used successfully by writers to uncover more information about their own writing.

Let's see how this technique can work for an author. Read the following writing prompt:

7 Write about the following statement in any way that you wish. 'Mrs Rachel Anderson has been a keen supporter for many years and has helped raise thousands of pounds.' Write up to one side of A4 paper.

This is quite a vague sentence that doesn't appear to give you much information. However, if you adopt an investigative approach and try to 'interview' or 'interrogate' the statement then you should be able to focus your imagination quite quickly. The more questions you can think to ask, the more answers you can imagine. These answers can then act as a springboard to kick-start your writing.

Imagine yourself in the role of an interviewer or newspaper journalist. What would you ask the given statement above in order to draw out more information? Here are ten possible questions:

1   *Who is Mrs Rachel Anderson?*
2   *How old is she?*
3   *Where does she live?*
4   *Who or what does she support?*
5   *When did she become a supporter?*
6   *Why did she become a supporter?*
7   *How much money has she raised over the years?*
8   *How has she raised the money?*
9   *What has the money been raised for?*
10   *Why is it important for the reader to know about Mrs Rachel Anderson?*

You may have been able to bring many more questions to mind but even with just these ten questions you can generate some imaginative answers, which could help to form a sound basis for your writing. For example:

1 Who is Mrs Rachel Anderson?	*A white-haired, short, plump lady.*
2 How old is she?	*94*
3 Where does she live?	*The Dell, Calcott, Reading.*
4 Who or what does she support?	*The National Children's Home.*
5 When did she become a supporter?	*1938*
6 Why did she become a supporter?	*She was looked after by the NCH when she was orphaned during the war.*
7 How much money has she raised over the years?	*£6,280*

8 How has she raised the money?	*She knits and sells baby clothes and blankets.*
9 What has the money been raised for?	*It has helped to fund temporary/ permanent homes for orphaned children or for children whose families couldn't look after them for a while.*
10 Why is it important for the reader to know about Mrs Rachel Anderson?	*Her actions show that anyone can make a difference, even by doing something small.*

Creating original answers like these should provide you with a realistic context in which you can set your writing, but why stop there? Any of these answers could lead to even more questions, more ideas and more details. For example, you now know that:

- *Mrs Anderson lives at The Dell, but who does she live with?*
- *she supports this charity, but does she support any others?*
- *she started raising funds in 1938, but why did she become involved in that particular year?*
- *she was orphaned during the war, but how did she come to be at the NCH?*
- *she knits and sells items to raise money, but why did she decide to raise funds in this way?*

When you have thought of answers to these queries, you will probably find that they will lead you to another set of questions and so on.

Whenever you are stuck for ideas, the 'interview and interrogate' method should help to set your imagination running. By engaging your investigative skills in this way, it shouldn't take long for you to produce pages full of ideas and information. In fact, don't be surprised if you find that you have more details than you need by the time you come to structure and develop your piece of writing. Remember in exams, though, to keep an eye on the time. It's easy to get carried away thinking up lots of questions and answers and then forget about leaving enough time to write up your ideas!

Top Tip

This method can be useful for all types of writing. For example, try using it to 'interview' your characters in a piece of fictional narrative or description in order to build up a fuller picture of them. Or, if you are writing a debate, imagine two people with opposing views and interview each of them to help create a balanced debate.

Top Tip

Why not become a journalist for a day and try out your interviewing techniques with your friends and family? Choose a topic, theme or event such as a memorable day, a favourite hobby or holiday or their childhood and think of one question to ask them about it. Write down their answer and then try to think of another question to ask them that is based on their response. Repeat this several times (until you have asked up to 20 questions, for example). Then read back through your notes and use them to write a recount, a story, or a magazine or newspaper article. When you have completed your writing, your interviewee might like to read the finished piece.

Now it's your turn!

Read the following newspaper quote:

Police arrested the man last Wednesday, but a court date has yet to be announced.

1 Write down 10 questions (and answers) about this sentence in your notebook.

2 Use these answers to generate another set of 10 questions and answers.

3 Referring to all of your answers, write a detailed paragraph about this event.

✓ Parent Tip

Looking at how tabloid and broadsheet newspapers write up a piece of news will give your child a real taste of journalistic writing, so encourage them to read as well as to write.

(c) Borrow and steal

This technique is similar to searching your memory as it relies on what you can remember. However, instead of trying to recall a personal experience, this method requires you to think about pieces of writing that you have already read.

If you find yourself stumped by a question prompt, it can be helpful to try and think about what it might have in common with something that has been previously written (either by you or someone else). For example, the topic of a fictional narrative or script prompt might enable you to 'steal' some ideas for a scene, a character or the general plot line from a storybook or play that you have read recently.

In fact, almost any source of writing could act as an ideas springboard or a writing framework for you; a fairy story, a newspaper report, a magazine article, a school textbook, a nursery rhyme, a play and a storybook are just a few examples. Let's have a look at how you might use this method based on the following writing prompt:

8 Adam Wright is a reporter. He is about to write up a news story for tomorrow's edition of his local neighbourhood watch magazine. The headline for his article is:

Clumsy cat-burglar caught catnapping in Chelsea!

Write the rest of Adam's article in no more than 250 words.

In this question, you have only been given a headline rather than a detailed outline of the story to start from. To help you generate some ideas about what might have happened you can try using the following 5-step plan on page 50–51.

| **1 Look at the title you have been given.** | → | *'Clumsy cat-burglar caught catnapping in Chelsea!'* What information can you work out from the article's headline? It suggests that it was possible to catch a thief because he/she was asleep. |

| **2 Choose a previous piece of writing that fits with the question topic.** | → | Can you think of a tale, article or rhyme, for example, that you have read which involves someone being caught because they fell asleep? How about the children's tale of 'Goldilocks and the Three Bears'? |

| **3 Outline the 'bare bones' of your chosen piece of writing.** | → | Briefly think about the basic events ('bare bones') of the piece of writing. |

1. Goldilocks stops outside the bears' house in the forest.
2. Seeing the house is empty, she walks in.
3. She tries three bowls of porridge and chooses the last one.
4. She tries out three chairs and chooses the last one, which breaks.
5. She goes upstairs, tries out three beds and falls asleep in the last one.
6. The three bears come home.
7. They know that someone has been eating their porridge, sitting in their chairs and sleeping in their beds.
8. They find Goldilocks asleep.
9. She wakes up to find the three bears standing over her.
10. She has been caught red-handed.

| **4 Apply the question prompt context.** | → | Assign the characters, setting, writing style and so on that are appropriate for the question. Hints for some of these features have been given to you in this example: |

- main characters: the cat-burglar
- setting: Chelsea
- writing style: a formal news article

Sometimes you may have to create some or all of these aspects yourself.

| **5 Use the 'bare bones' to build the steps of your own writing.** | → | Now use some or all of the 'bare bones' from your chosen reference text to help you develop the structure and events for your own piece of writing. |

'Clumsy cat-burglar caught catnapping in Chelsea!' by Adam Wright

(1) At lunchtime yesterday Ben Parks, an amateur thief, stood outside Chelsea's Bank Hotel. **(2)** He waited until the receptionist left for lunch and then wandered across the lobby towards the ground floor suites. **(3)** The first two doors he tried were locked but the third one opened easily. **(4)** Finding nothing of value in the bathroom or around the lounge area, Mr Parks proceeded to ransack the wardrobe. His efforts were quickly rewarded with a wallet, a set of car keys and a passport.

(5) Fortunately for Mr Jackson, the room's occupant, Mr Parks's exit was prevented at that moment by some housekeeping staff starting work in the corridor. As the windows in the bathroom and the lounge offered no means of escape, Mr Parks opted to relax on the luxurious king-size bed and wait for them to finish.

 The secrets of writing

(6) Mr Jackson returned to his room shortly after lunch. **(7)** He noticed instantly that his room and belongings had been disturbed and immediately called hotel security. **(8)** When the security officers inspected Mr Jackson's whole suite, they were amazed to find the culprit sleeping soundly at the crime scene.

(9) A startled Mr Parks soon awoke to find two security guards and a very angry hotel resident looming over him. **(10)** Found with wallet and keys still clutched in his hand, this bungling burglar will now have plenty of time to daydream – in a police cell!

Remember – a burglar could be looking at your property right now, so lock your doors and windows every time you leave the house.

Can you see how the 10 basic facts from the tale of 'Goldilocks and the Three Bears' have been 'borrowed' to create and organise the ideas for a response to the question prompt? Following the 'borrow and steal' technique can be a sure way of kick-starting your ideas and of quickly developing a basic structure for your writing. However, if you are still unsure of how this method works, try comparing the 10 numbered sections of the news article in step 5 to the 'bare bones' outline shown in step 3 above.

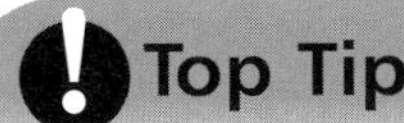

Top Tip

Avoid copying the characters, events and so on too closely from a piece of writing or repeating phrases word for word. It is fine to draw on the general plot outline and structure of another source but you must then bring in your own ideas and imagination to make your piece of writing your own. You could lose marks if you have copied an existing text too closely.

Now it's your turn!

Choose one of the following writing prompts and then use the 'borrow and steal 5-step plan' to develop your answer.

- Write a short story about friendship. Write up to two sides of A4 paper. (Stories such as Enid Blyton's *Famous Five* series or Anne Fine's *The Tulip Touch* could be useful starting points here.)

- Write the opening scene from a play entitled *Never Judge a Book by its Cover*. Write up to two sides of A4 paper. (Stories such as the Disney classic *Beauty and the Beast*, Michael Morpurgo's *Gentle Giant* or Ted Hughes's *The Iron Man* could give you some ideas here.)

- Write a 300-word article for an animal welfare magazine that discusses the 'ideal pet'. (RSPCA leaflets, guides on looking after pets or poetry collections such as T. S. Eliot's *Old Possum's Book of Practical Cats* could spark off some ideas here.)

Once you have written your answer, ask someone to try and guess which piece of writing you have 'borrowed' some ideas from.

● Create a plan

So you now know which question you are going to answer, you have thought about what format and writing style are required for the task and have some good ideas, but you're not sure how to start. This is where you need a foolproof plan.

Often, writing exams give you a few minutes to read and plan before you need to start writing, and this time should be used carefully to outline the structure and content of your response. If specific planning time is not given, then make sure you allow yourself enough time to generate, organise and shape your ideas before you begin writing.

There are no firm rules for how long you should plan a piece of writing but, as a rough guide – try to spend around one fifth (or even up to half) of your time on the planning stage. Often, the most well thought out, organised, logical and fluent pieces of writing come from clearly developed plans.

All writing tasks should be easier to complete when you have a plan to follow and, although no two writing tasks will be the same, you can sketch out a plan for any type of task. The format and focus of your plan are likely to differ slightly depending on the type of task you are doing, so let's have a look at how to plan an answer for some of the most common types of writing task.

(a) Planning a debate

Here is a useful 4-step strategy for planning a response to a debate question:

> **1 Look at what you have been given.**
>
> What topic or issue does the question raise?
>
> Do you have any inspiration such as a piece of given text to refer to?

> **2 Note down your thoughts, ideas and key points.**
>
> Draw a pair of spider diagrams and label one 'for' and the other 'against', or the first 'positive' and the second 'negative', or 'agree' and 'disagree', or 'yes' and 'no' and so on. Using two diagrams will enable you to clearly group similar ideas together for each side of the debate you are going to write.
>
> Try to make sure that for every positive point you have noted you have thought of a related negative point, as this will help you to develop a balanced argument. If you have a piece of given text to refer to, re-read it and underline the keywords. Place these keywords, along with your own ideas, on the relevant spider diagram.

Top Tip

These 6 keywords can be helpful here!

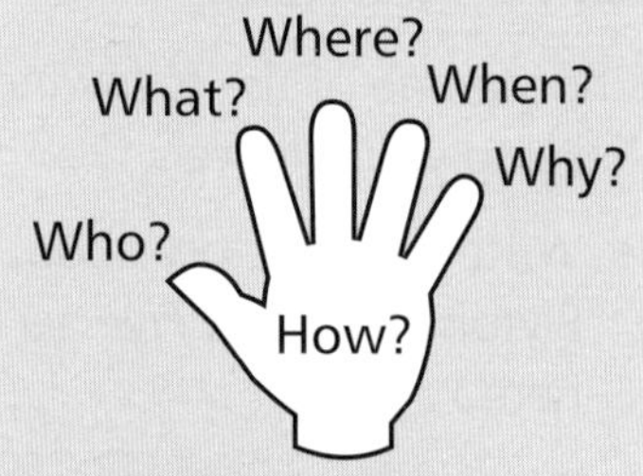

> **3 Organise your points.**
>
> Read through the points you have made and then number each one in the order you want to include them in your answer. Your points should follow on from each other in a logical sequence to ensure that your argument flows easily and makes sense to the reader.
>
> Ordering your points and grouping them into paragraphs will ensure that you know what you are going to say and where you are going to say it. Numbering each point will also make sure you don't miss any out as you write.
>
> Whenever you swap from one side of a discussion to another, remember to link your points with connective words or phrases: however, on the one hand ... but on the other hand, some people might think that ... , in comparison, meanwhile and so on.

Top Tip

Remember to write in paragraphs so that your reader can follow your argument.

Presenting one side of the debate in full, then explaining the opposite viewpoint is likely to make your response easier to read than if you continually switch between opposing views.

4 **Draw your conclusion.**

When you have written down all of the points you want to include, read through them and make a note of which side of the debate you agree with most.

Deciding your conclusion before you write should help you to order the points you want to make and keep your debate focused.

Here is a typical debate prompt:

1 Is space travel a good thing? Explain your answer, writing no more than one side of A4 paper.

A writing plan for this question might look something like this:

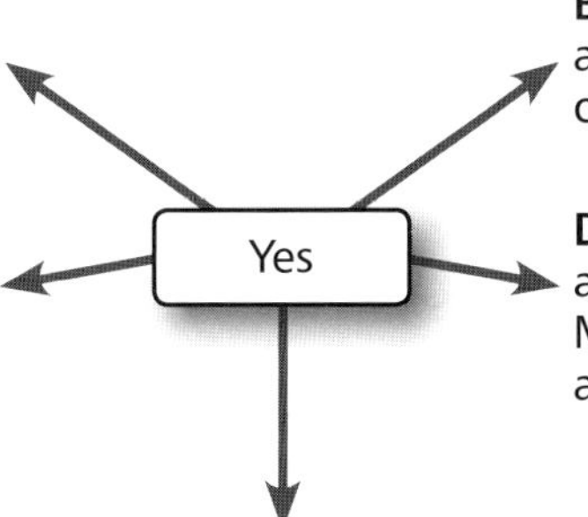

A We might find out more about how life on Earth began.

B If we could build on the Moon or another star we could go on holiday or even live in outer space.

C Other countries have space programmes so if we didn't continue with it in the UK, we would fall behind with scientific discoveries and new technologies.

D It would be exciting to see if we are alone or if there really is life on Mars or any other planet – to find aliens would be great.

E We might find out more about the cause and effect of global warming that could help us work towards practical solutions on Earth.

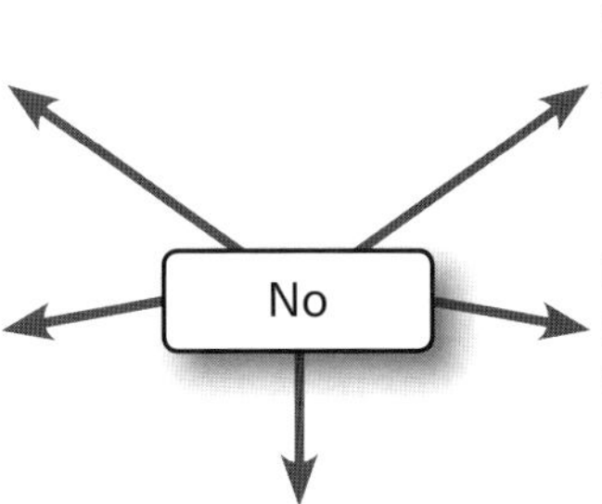

F Space travel is dangerous and there have been a number of accidents or disasters with space shuttles in the past.

G Space travel is only ever likely to involve a small, elite group of people – not the general public.

H The costs are huge. The money could be better spent on more important areas that will benefit everyone, such as hospitals or schools.

I If we disturbed a hostile race, they might decide to invade Earth. Could we protect ourselves?

J It pollutes outer space, adding to the scale of the global warming problem. More travel = more pollution.

There is rarely one correct viewpoint for a debate writing prompt and no strict rules to follow about the order in which you should present your points. So once you have created your plan, and have decided whether you are for or against the given question or statement, you can begin writing up your response.

If you have decided that you are 'for', 'in favour of' or support the issue raised in the prompt, then you may choose to present the reader with all of your positive points first. This could help to encourage them into a positive frame of mind before you discuss the argument from the alternative viewpoint. Your conclusion could then draw the reader back to a positive opinion by summarising the key points that you outlined in the first part of your debate. Following this structure would mean that the reader would be left with a positive thought and would also clearly be able to see which side of the argument you favoured.

So, to write a positive response for the prompt given above, you might choose to order your notes as follows:

1 A	6 F
2 D	7 I
3 B	8 G
4 C	9 H
5 E	10 J

leading to a concluding statement such as:

In conclusion, I feel that space travel is a good thing because it may help us to understand how the Earth began and this information could then assist us in solving future problems.

However, if you decided that you were 'against' or 'not in favour' of the given debate topic, then you may choose to write all of your negative points first before presenting the opposing view and then finally drawing your reader back to a negative viewpoint in your conclusion.

So, for the example debate prompt above, this might mean that you would choose to order your points as follows:

1 G	6 A
2 H	7 D
3 I	8 C
4 J	9 B
5 F	10 E

leading to a concluding statement such as:

In conclusion, I feel that space travel is not a good thing because the costs in terms of money, pollution and danger to human life are too great.

Many people find that it is easier to discuss one side of a debate first before turning to consider the opposing viewpoint. However, you may prefer to present your reader with a mix of views throughout your writing. There is nothing wrong with this but it can be a bit more tricky to structure, as you need to make sure that opposing points follow on sensibly from each other. You should also try to remember that if you switch from one side of an argument to the other *too* regularly, it can be hard for the reader to follow your writing.

If you were to follow this style of writing for the example debate prompt above, then you might choose to order your points like this:

1 A	6 G
2 D	7 B
3 I	8 E
4 C	9 J
5 H	10 F

leading to a concluding statement that could be either positive or negative.

Remember that an examiner will not be looking for the 'one right answer' to a debate. As long as you present a logical and clearly supported argument, you can feel confident in your writing – whatever view you take.

(b) Planning a recount or report

You can follow a similar 4-step plan for recount and report prompts:

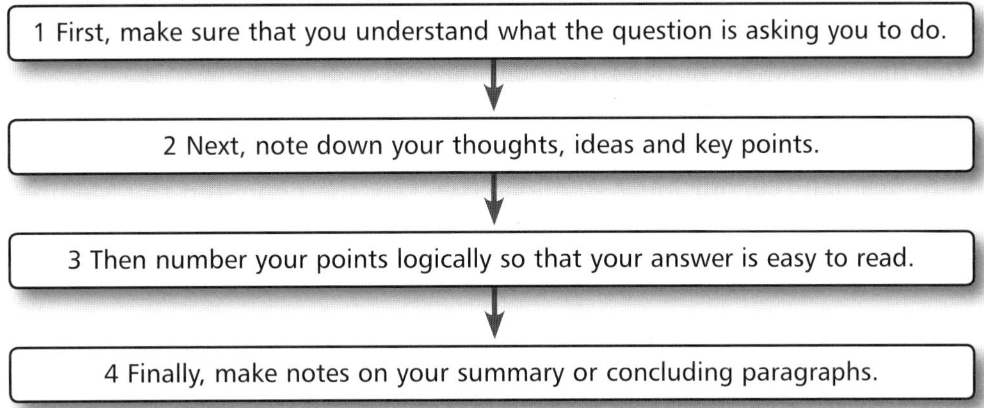

The differences with this type of question relate to how you note down your ideas and the way in which you order them. A spider diagram is often the best format for planning an answer to this type of question but, unlike a debate prompt, you should only need to draw one.

As you will be writing a report or recount of an event you will not need to order your points in relation to opposing viewpoints. Instead, it might be more appropriate to order your points chronologically to create an accurate timeline of events; or in order of preference (from your most to least favourite, for example); or in topics.

Look at this recount prompt:

2 Describe a travel journey that you have been on. Write no more than 300 words.

Preparing a writing plan for a recount prompt, like the one shown below, will enable you to write a flowing account that takes each point in turn and offers a structured and logical progression that is easy to read and follow.

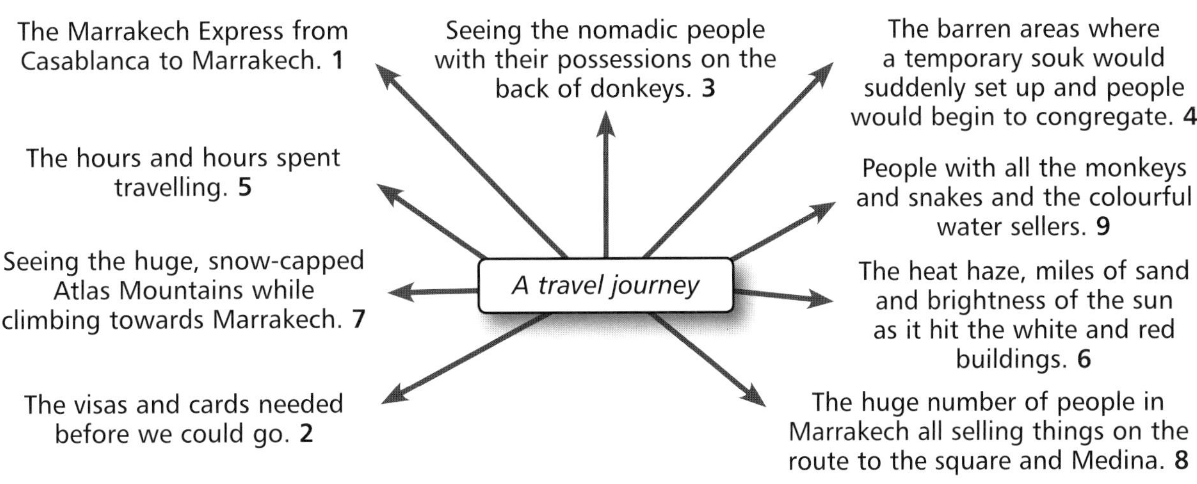

Quick timeline check:

Top Tip

Once the diagram is complete, you may wish to double-check the order of your points, particularly if they relate to a timeline, to make sure that you are happy with the sequence of events that they show.

1. This is the journey about to be described, so it should come first as a title.
2. This was the key thing we had to do before beginning the journey, so it should come next.
3. The people – we noticed them first through the train window after starting the journey, so they are the next point.
4. Next, we saw the makeshift souks.
5. Then we talked about how long the journey was taking.
6. At our first break, we noticed the heat haze etc.
7. We reached the Atlas Mountains in the next stage of the journey.
8. After that, we saw the people making their way into the square in Marrakech.
9. And then finally, as our journey ended, we saw the people in the Medina.

Summary points:

- *The travel journey was an amazing experience as it was so different.*
- *This was not just a physical journey but a dream that my parents had always had and it was just as good as they had imagined.*
- *The experience has made me want to travel a lot when I am older.*

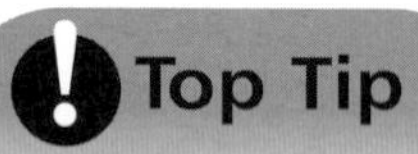

Top Tip

If you are writing a time sequence, putting points into chronological order makes sense. This system works well for so many writing questions, from a restaurant review to a recount of a particular day. It makes your writing flow logically and allows your reader to be taken along a journey or an experience with you.

(c) Planning a description

Again, as for the last two prompt types, the same 4-step strategy can be followed for descriptive pieces of writing. When ordering your points for descriptions, as for some recounts and reports, it is best to group ideas together that relate to the same topic or theme.

You might identify similar points in your notes by:

- *underlining them in the same colour*
- *noting down a key next to the diagram*
- *numbering them in order.*

Here is a typical description prompt:

3 Think of a person that you know and describe them in 250 words.

A writing plan for this question might look like this:

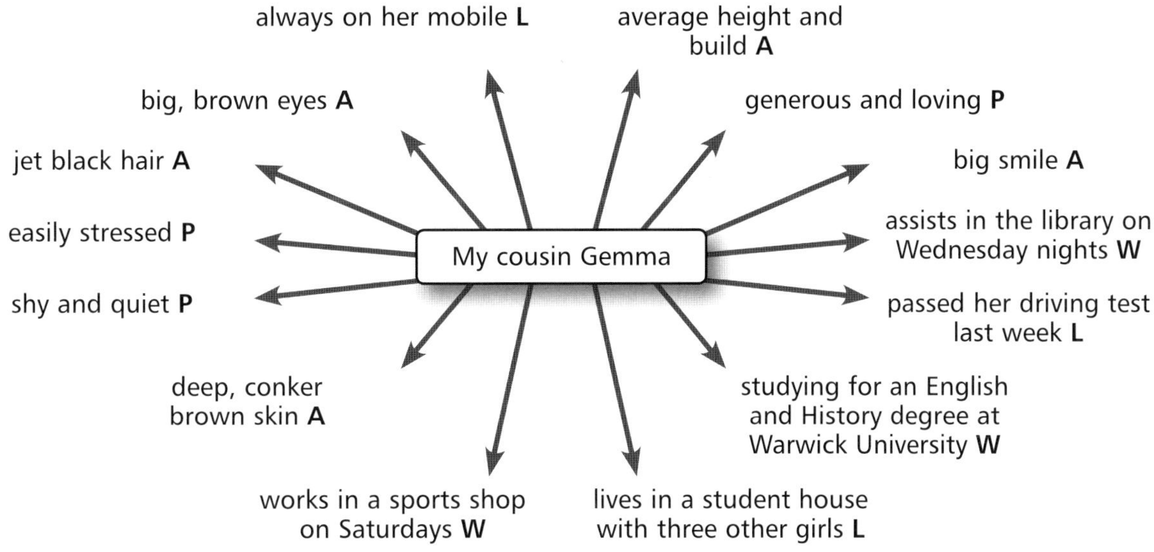

Key

A = appearance   **L** = lifestyle   **P** = personality   **W** = work

Summary points:

- *Although we're related, Gemma is very different from me in many ways.*
- *Two things we do have in common are our accents and sense of humour.*
- *I've chosen to describe Gemma because she's my favourite cousin; she is great to be with and I'm glad we're family.*

All of the points shown in the spider diagram have been grouped into four topic areas as shown in the key. If you collate your ideas in this way, you can then use the key as a basis to organise your notes into paragraphs.
For example:

Paragraph 1: all points relating to appearance
Paragraph 2: all points relating to personality
Paragraph 3: all points relating to lifestyle
Paragraph 4: all points relating to work
Paragraph 5: all summary points

Following this format will help to ensure that, when you come to write your response, your ideas will be grouped logically and will follow a clear structure.

If you are writing a descriptive piece, try to think of groups that your points could be divided into. For example, describing your favourite author might make you think of: characters the author uses, places the books are set in, plot lines or how an adventure is worked through, or what key aspects make this author different from other writers.

d) Planning a narrative

Fictional narrative writing often requires a more detailed planning process than the previous three prompt types. This is because your writing will rely on your own imagination and creativity. To ensure that you show your story writing at its best, start by producing a clear outline of your ideas using a strategy such as the 5-point plan shown overleaf.

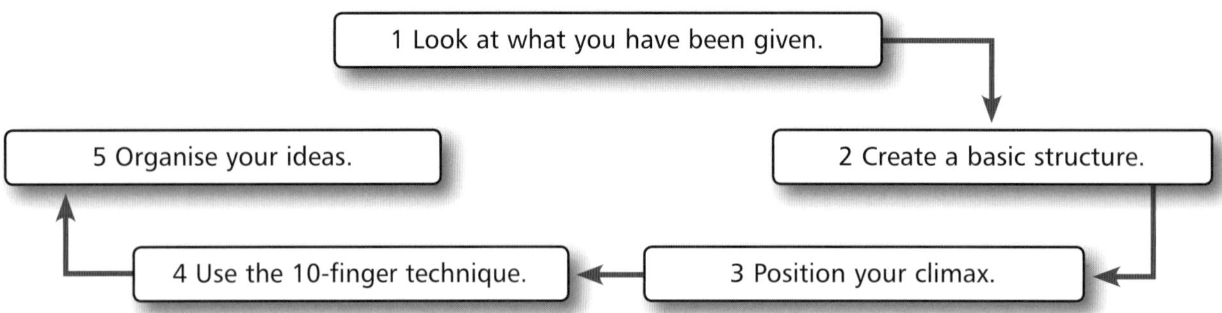

To see how this planning process might work, let's look at it in the context of the following narrative prompt:

4 Write imaginatively about the following title: 'The Lucky Escape!' Write up to two sides of A4 paper.

1 Look at what you have been given

When reading the prompt, first ask yourself questions such as: *What topic or issue is the title prompt based on? Has a piece of text been given that you could take any ideas from?*

In this example, only a title has been given but it presents quite an open topic that could send your imagination off in many different directions. For example, it might immediately spark off some basic ideas about who or what could be escaping, where the escape could be from/to, why and how the escape has happened and so on.

Make sure you note down any rough thoughts that come to mind at this point.

2 Create a basic structure

Once you have noted down some initial thoughts based on the given topic/title prompt, try to add a basic structure to your ideas. Remember that every story, even a simple one, should have:

- *a beginning – an opening sentence or paragraph that sets the scene for the action*
- *a middle – several paragraphs that develop the storyline*
- *an end – a final section that draws the action to a close, often providing a resolution to a problem encountered during the story.*

Keeping these basic elements in mind as you write your notes will help you to think about how your story should develop and how it will take the reader on a journey from beginning to end.

To help you 'see' how your ideas could form the clear basis for a story, you might find it useful to lay your thoughts out on a simple timeline, like the one shown below.

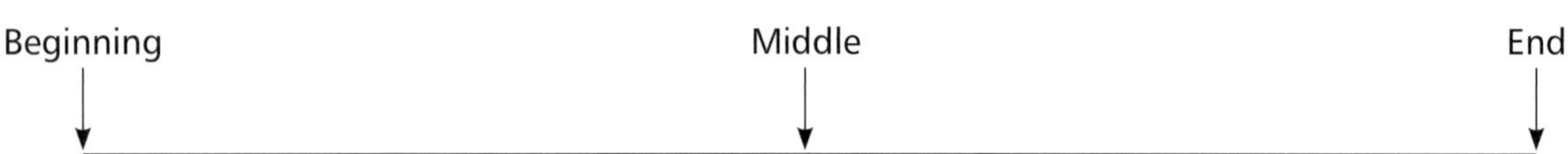

Using this technique can help you to focus on what should happen when and where in the plot. It can also help you to start splitting your ideas into groups, which you can then use as a basis for the paragraphs in your writing.

So, for the given title prompt above, a basic timeline might look something like this:

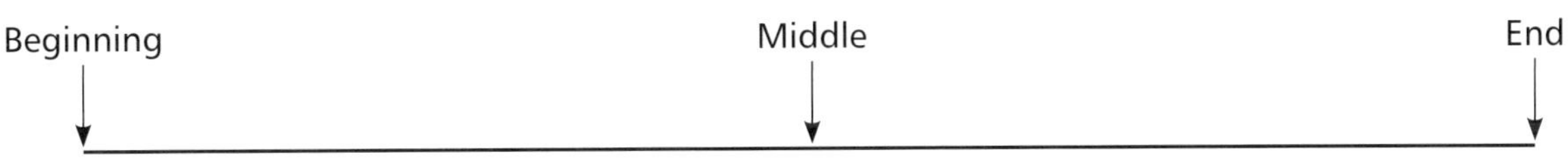

Beginning	Middle	End
1 Samira loves animals. 2 She was given a baby rabbit for Christmas. 3 It soon became clear that he had a very inquisitive nature; his nose was always twitching! 4 Samira called him Sniffy.	5 When she goes to feed him, the cage is open; Sniffy has escaped. 6 Suddenly, Samira spots Sniffy in the neighbours' garden, nibbling the grass in front of the dog's kennel. 7 He must have burrowed under the fence!	8 She rushes round to the neighbours' house to rescue Sniffy from Fido! 9 Mrs Goodall explains that Fido is unwell, so Sniffy is in no danger. 10 Samira picks up Sniffy and takes him home, remembering to lock the hutch door this time!

These simple notes about Sniffy's 'lucky escape' tell the story in a 'linear' style; the events are written in a straight line, starting with when Samira first had Sniffy and finishing with him being placed back in his hutch after his adventure. However, as we shall see in the next step of this plan, your story does not have to follow this type of linear pattern.

3 Position your climax

A well-chosen opening can create drama and grab the reader's attention immediately, so think carefully about the point at which you bring the reader into your story. Do you want to raise their interest gradually, surprise them in the middle of the action or shock them from the start?

Some of the best stories, rather than following a linear approach, start at the end or in the middle of the action and then take the reader backwards so that they can see how the events unfolded. To show you how a story can unravel from different starting points, here are two more simple timelines that tell the same details about Sniffy but which follow different time sequences:

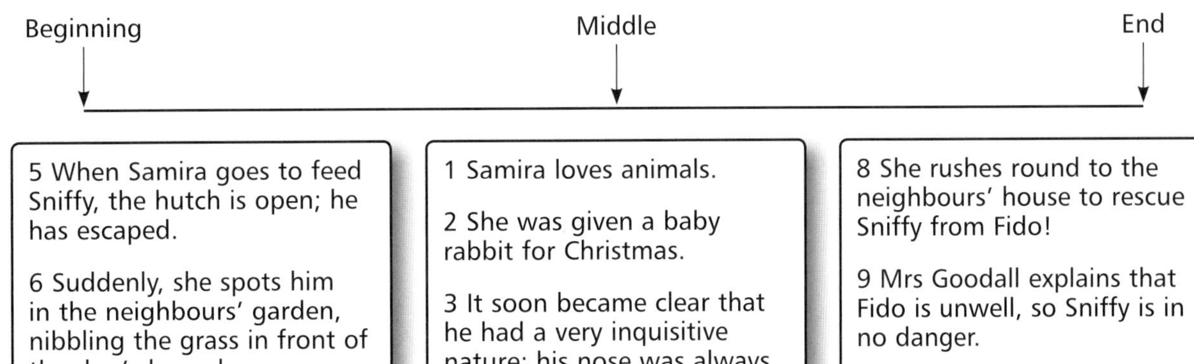

Beginning	Middle	End
5 When Samira goes to feed Sniffy, the hutch is open; he has escaped. 6 Suddenly, she spots him in the neighbours' garden, nibbling the grass in front of the dog's kennel. 7 He must have burrowed under the fence!	1 Samira loves animals. 2 She was given a baby rabbit for Christmas. 3 It soon became clear that he had a very inquisitive nature; his nose was always twitching! 4 Samira called him Sniffy.	8 She rushes round to the neighbours' house to rescue Sniffy from Fido! 9 Mrs Goodall explains that Fido is unwell, so Sniffy is in no danger. 10 Samira picks up Sniffy and takes him home, remembering to lock the hutch door this time!

Beginning   Middle   End

8 Samira rushes round to the neighbours' house to rescue Sniffy from Fido!

9 Mrs Goodall explains that Fido is unwell, so Sniffy is in no danger.

10 Samira picks up Sniffy and takes him home; remembering to lock the hutch door this time!

1 Samira loves animals.

2 She was given a baby rabbit for Christmas.

3 It soon became clear that he had a very inquisitive nature; his nose was always twitching!

4 Samira called him Sniffy.

5 When she went to feed Sniffy, the hutch was open; he had escaped.

6 Suddenly, Samira spotted him in the neighbours' garden, nibbling the grass in front of the dog's kennel.

7 He must have burrowed under the fence!

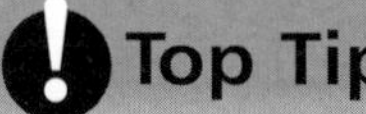

Top Tip

Memory flashbacks are a useful technique for showing the reader the events that took place prior to the starting point of the story.

Your choice of starting position, and the effect you want to create with it, often relates to where you position the climax of your story. All stories need an interesting, exciting or shocking event that will catch the reader's attention. This main focal point is called the climax; the highest or most dramatic point of your narrative. It could be in the form of a dilemma, a challenge, or a thrilling discovery, for example.

Often the climax is found near the middle of a story, with the first half of the plot building towards it and then working towards a solution by the end. However, as we have seen above, stories do not have to be linear, which means that a climax can also be placed at the beginning or the end of a storyline. In the first timeline for 'A Lucky Escape!' the climax (Sniffy's escape) forms the middle section of the story. However, in the second timeline the climax opens the story, while in the third timeline it is left until the end. This shows that even a simple story can be told with drama, so think carefully about what and where the climax should be when planning your writing.

If you are not sure where to place your climax or what effect you want to create, it might help to 'draw' the flow of the plot. Look at the following three lines. Each line represents one of the simple nursery rhymes on the next page. The position of the climax has been marked for each one.

Line A

Line B

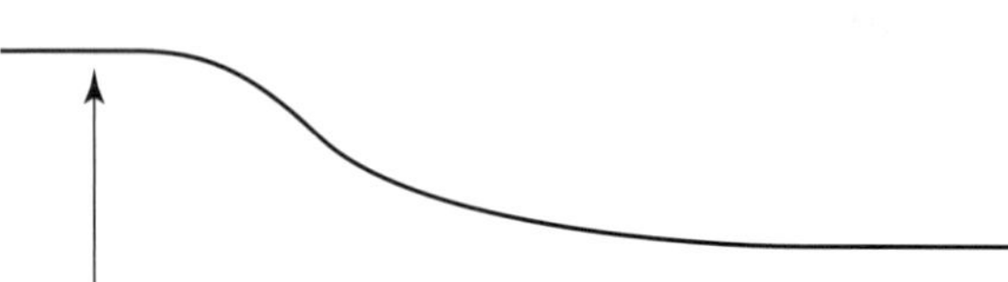

The dramatic climax is here at the beginning.

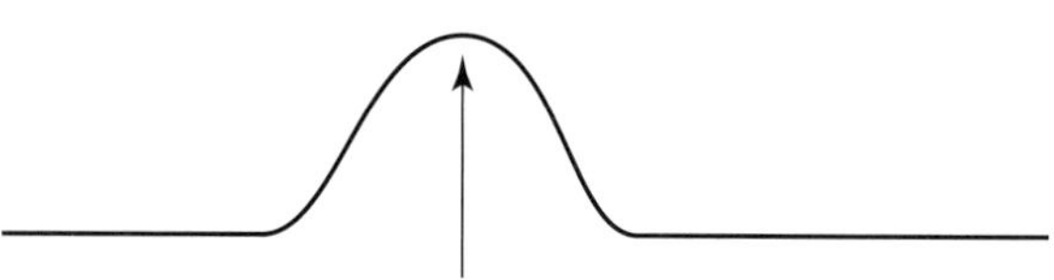

The dramatic climax is here at the middle.

Line C

The dramatic climax is here at the end.

Can you match the correct line to its nursery rhyme?

Pop goes the Weasel

Half a pound of tuppenny
  rice
Half a pound of treacle
That's the way the money
  goes
POP! Goes the weasel.

Line _____

Humpty Dumpty

Humpty Dumpty sat on a
  wall,
Humpty Dumpty had a great
  fall!
All the King's horses
And all the King's men
Couldn't put Humpty
Together again.

Line _____

Little Bo-Peep

Little Bo-Peep has lost her
  sheep
And doesn't know where to
  find them.
Leave them alone and they
  will come home
Wagging their tails behind
  them.

Line _____

All writing needs to 'rise and fall' with anticipation of drama, action, a climax and a resolution. Keeping high levels of drama throughout can be exhausting for your reader, but not including enough drama can make your writing uninteresting and boring to read. Planning the positions of your dramatic moments is therefore vital when writing narrative text.

In order to create drama effectively, you also need to clearly plan out who it involves. The next stage of this plan shows you a quick and effective way of generating ideas about your characters – particularly useful when planning time is limited in exams!

4 Use the 10-finger technique

Including one or more characters can provide your story with substance and create a sense of realism. It will also make it easier for your reader to engage with the events being described and to identify more closely with those involved. However, you won't have very long to scope out the details of your characters, so don't get carried away thinking up a whole host of them!

Once you have decided on the number of characters your story *needs*, imagine yourself as each character and ask yourself some or all of the following 10 questions:

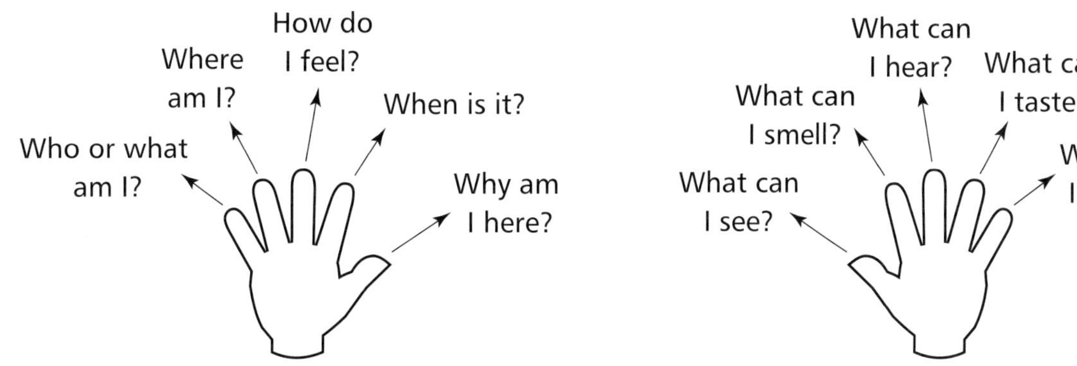

1 **Who or what am I?** Briefly describe your
characters. You might include details such as:
name, age, appearance, any unique features,
personality and relationships or connections with
other characters.

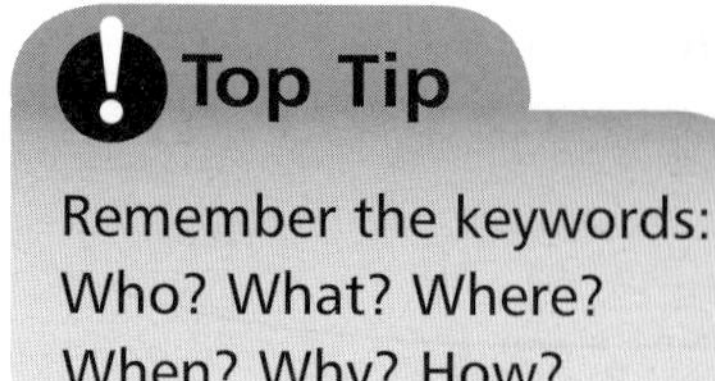

Remember the keywords:
Who? What? Where?
When? Why? How?

2 **Where am I?** Building a picture of the
surroundings is vital in creating atmosphere, so
try to include a short scale of detail such as:
in England $\longrightarrow$ in Chester $\longrightarrow$ in a bungalow $\longrightarrow$ in a bedroom $\longrightarrow$ in bed.

3 **How do I feel?** Descriptions of emotions can help the reader to understand a
character and to empathise more easily with their situation. So try to include
details of, for example, how a character feels (happy, sad, disappointed,
frightened and so on); what has caused them to feel like this and whether they
have felt like this before.

4 **When is it?** Explaining when something is happening will help to place
events in context so you might, for example, include details of the time of
day (morning, two o'clock, evening, midnight and so on), the day (Monday,
Saturday) or date (is it significant, a birthday perhaps?) or the time of year
(spring, summer, September, Christmas).

5 **Why am I here?** Describing why and how a character is involved in the events
will help to explain their position in the plot, again adding to the overall
context of the storyline. Try to provide details such as why they are there, what
they are doing and perhaps what they were doing before they entered the
story.

6 **What can I see?** Describing what a character is looking at can help the reader
to 'see' the description, so try to include details of elements such as buildings,
weather, people, animals and scenery.

7 **What can I smell?** Introducing the sense of smell in a description can also
create a strong image for the reader and help them to imagine the scene they
are reading about. Perhaps a character can smell the scent of flowers such as
lavender, lilies or honeysuckle or newly cut grass, burning wood or dirty
sewers!

8 **What can I hear?** Think of what might be within earshot of each character
and what noise it would make. Describing a range of sounds will encourage the
reader to use their sense of hearing to develop a scene, so you might include
details of, for example, animal calls or birdsong, talking, music, the television,
traffic, the weather, the sea or even silence.

9 **What can I taste?** If a character eats or drinks something, imagine what it
would taste like. Sweet? Sour? Bitter? Salty? Spicy? Delicious? Describing it in
detail will bring the experience to life.

10 **What can I touch?** If a character touches an object, try to include details of the
material it is made from (glass, wood, plastic, metal, fabric, paper and so on)
as well as what it feels like (smooth, rough, sharp, blunt, slimy, ice-cold, warm).
Describing something with such detail will make the object more 'real' for the
reader.

We have seen that creating a timeline can help your story move on from one event to
the next and that careful positioning of the climax will generate the key dramatic effect.
Following the 10-finger technique will help to decorate the events with detail, ensuring

that the journey taken by the reader will be engaging and that they will want to keep reading through to the end.

So, using the 10-finger technique, some of the details in the basic outline of 'The Lucky Escape!' could be expanded as follows:

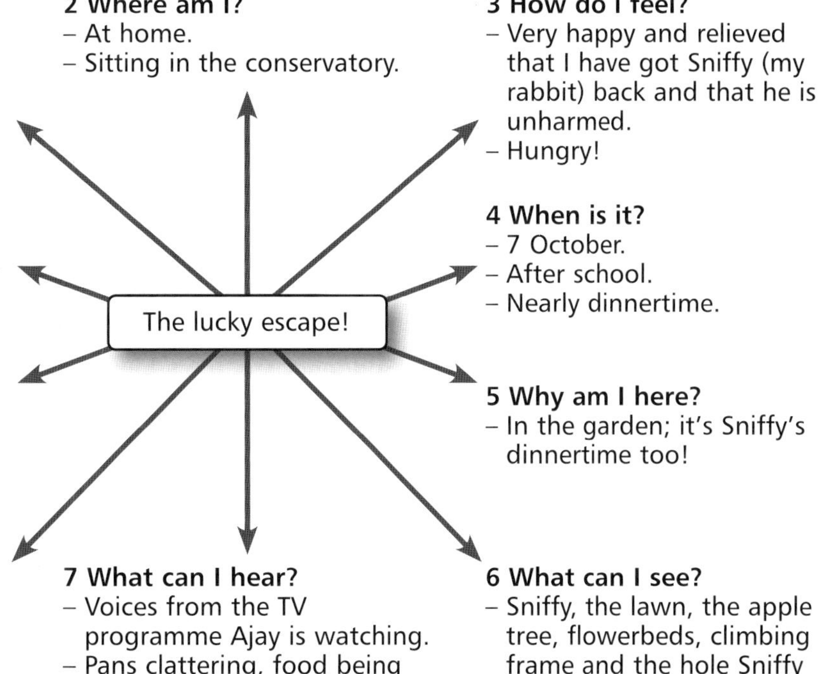

As with the plans for the previous prompt types, once you have noted down all of your key points you should organise them carefully to ensure that the structure of your storyline is clear and logical to follow. The final step in the plan looks at some ways you might do this.

5 Organise your ideas

You may choose to group your ideas into paragraphs, as we saw with description prompts, or you might prefer to number or letter the individual points and then place them in the appropriate places on your plot timeline. This will help you to 'see' what you are going to write as well as where you are going to include it.

Here is an example of how the second basic timeline about Samira might be expanded and juggled around to incorporate the ideas generated by the 10-finger technique above.

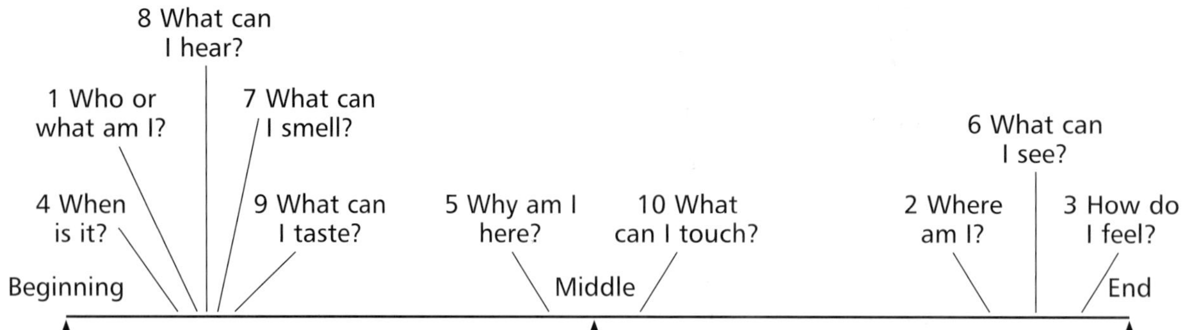

The labels along the timeline read:

8 What can I hear?

1 Who or what am I?   7 What can I smell?

6 What can I see?

4 When is it?   9 What can I taste?   5 Why am I here?   10 What can I touch?   2 Where am I?   3 How do I feel?

Beginning   Middle   End

Beginning

1 When is it? (7 October/after school/nearly dinnertime)

2 Who or what am I? (Samira/nine years old/long, black hair/blue shalwar kameez)

3 What can I hear? (TV voices/pans clattering/chopping)

4 What can I smell? (spices/vegetables/curry)

5 What can I taste? (imagining vegetable curry)

Middle

6 Why am I here? (to feed Sniffy)

7 What can I touch? (recall Sniffy's softness and warmth)

8 When Samira goes to feed Sniffy, the hutch is open; he has escaped.

9 Suddenly, she spots him in the neighbours' garden in front of the dog's kennel.

10 He must have burrowed under the fence!

11 Samira loves animals.

12 She was given a baby rabbit for Christmas.

13 It soon became clear that he had a very inquisitive nature; his nose was always twitching!

14 Samira called him Sniffy.

End

15 She rushes round to the neighbours' house to rescue Sniffy from Fido!

16 Mrs Goodall explains that Fido is unwell, so Sniffy is in no danger.

17 Samira picks up Sniffy and takes him home; remembering to lock the hutch door this time!

18 Where am I? (at home/in the conservatory)

19 What can I see? (Sniffy/garden view/Mum)

20 How do I feel? (happy/relieved/hungry)

Grouping your ideas together, whether in paragraphs or as notes along a timeline, should make it easier to visualise the overall structure of your writing. This, in turn, will make it faster to write up your ideas in full for a piece of fictional narrative.

Top Tip

You may be able to think of lots of ideas for your piece of narrative writing, but remember that you don't need to include all of them. Only add in the details that you think your story needs and that are likely to be of most interest to your reader.

e Planning a diary entry

You can follow a similar type of planning process for a diary entry as for other types of recounts and reports:

The secrets of writing

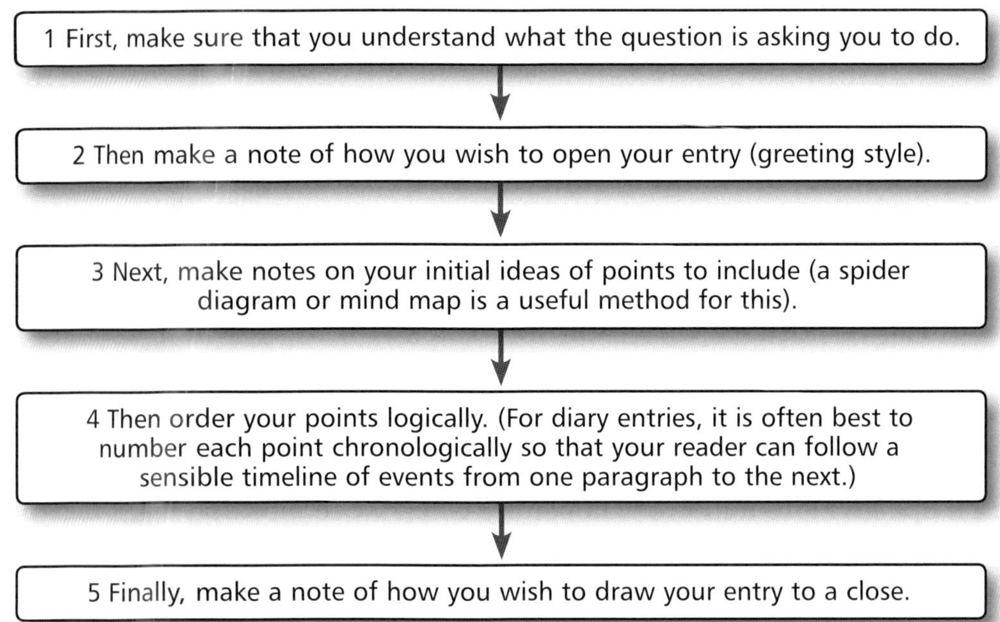

Here is a typical diary prompt:

5 Erica has become separated from her husband and two children following an earthquake. She was rescued from the hotel they were staying in and is now in a shelter with many other injured tourists and local people. She has a few belongings with her, one of which is her holiday diary. Write Erica's diary entry for that night, describing her experience. Write up to 350 words.

Using a plan like the one outlined above, your notes for this question might look like this:

Date: Wednesday 21 October 2009
Time: 9.30pm
Opening: Dear Diary,

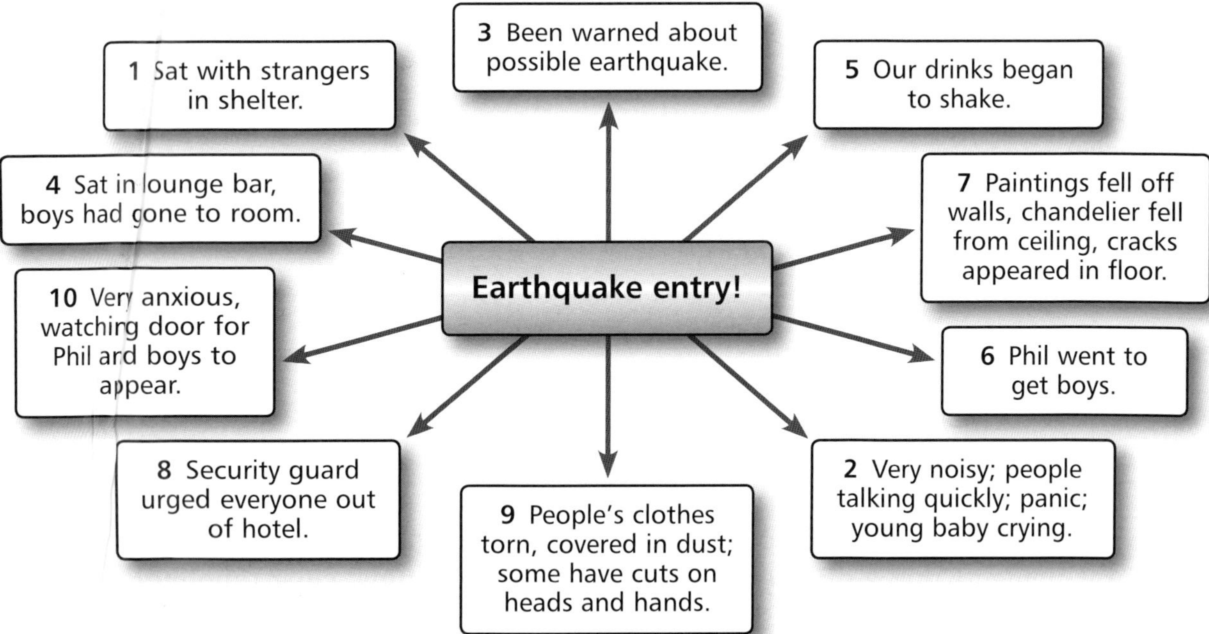

Timeline check:

1 This is where I am now.
2 This is what I can hear now.
3 This is what we had been told before travelling.
4 This is where we were when it started.
5 This is what we noticed first.
6 This is when we got separated.
7 This happened as the earthquake got stronger.
8 This happened next.
9 This is what I can see now.
10 This is how I feel now.

Closing: I'll update more tomorrow, hopefully when we're all safely back together, Erica.

If you find it difficult to remember that diary entries usually follow a standard layout, you may prefer to write your planning notes on a blank diary template such as the one shown below:

Date:	Time:
Opening greeting: (Dear ... Hi! ... etc.)	
Paragraph 1: (introduce context of diary entry)	• • • • •
Paragraph 2: (add details of events; link points with time connectives, e.g. while, first, afterwards, next, etc.) **Paragraph 3:** (as above) (and so on ...)	• • • • • • • • • •
Closing/sign-off: (Bye for now ... More later ... etc.)	

Following a template like this should help to ensure that you include all of the key structural elements that a diary entry needs (e.g. date, opening, clear timeline, paragraphs and closing).

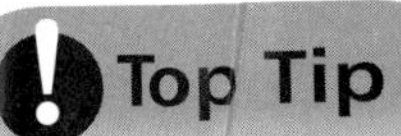

Top Tip

If you're stuck for ideas when writing a diary entry, try using the 'interrogate and interview' method (see pages 46–49) or the '10-finger technique' (see pages 61–64).

(f) Planning a letter

The thought process used for planning diaries can also be adapted when preparing to write letters.

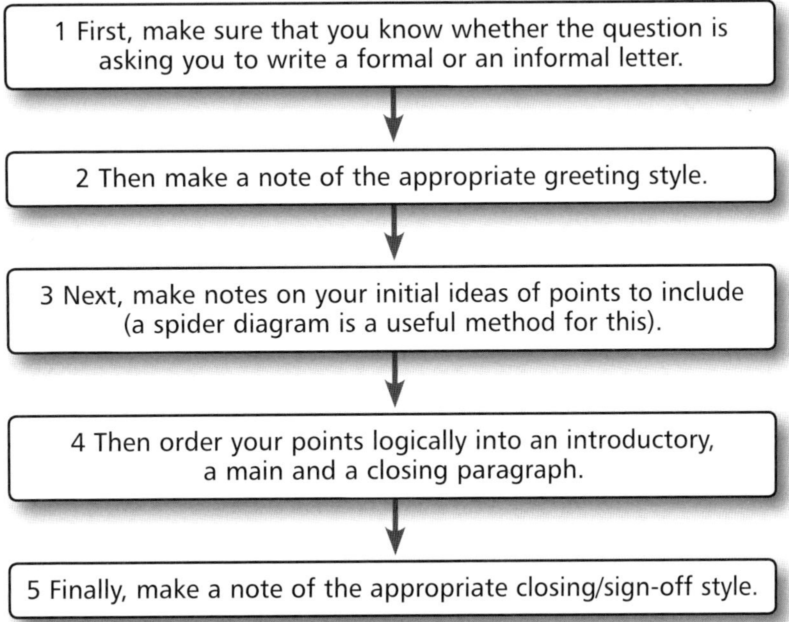

Here is an example letter prompt:

6 The local council is proposing to close your community library and reuse the building for more council offices. Write to your local MP, expressing your views on why the library should remain open. The main content of the letter should be no more than 350 words.

Following the suggested plan above, you might write out your notes like this:

- Writing to MP = formal letter
- Formal greeting style = Dear [make up a name] or [Sir/Madam]

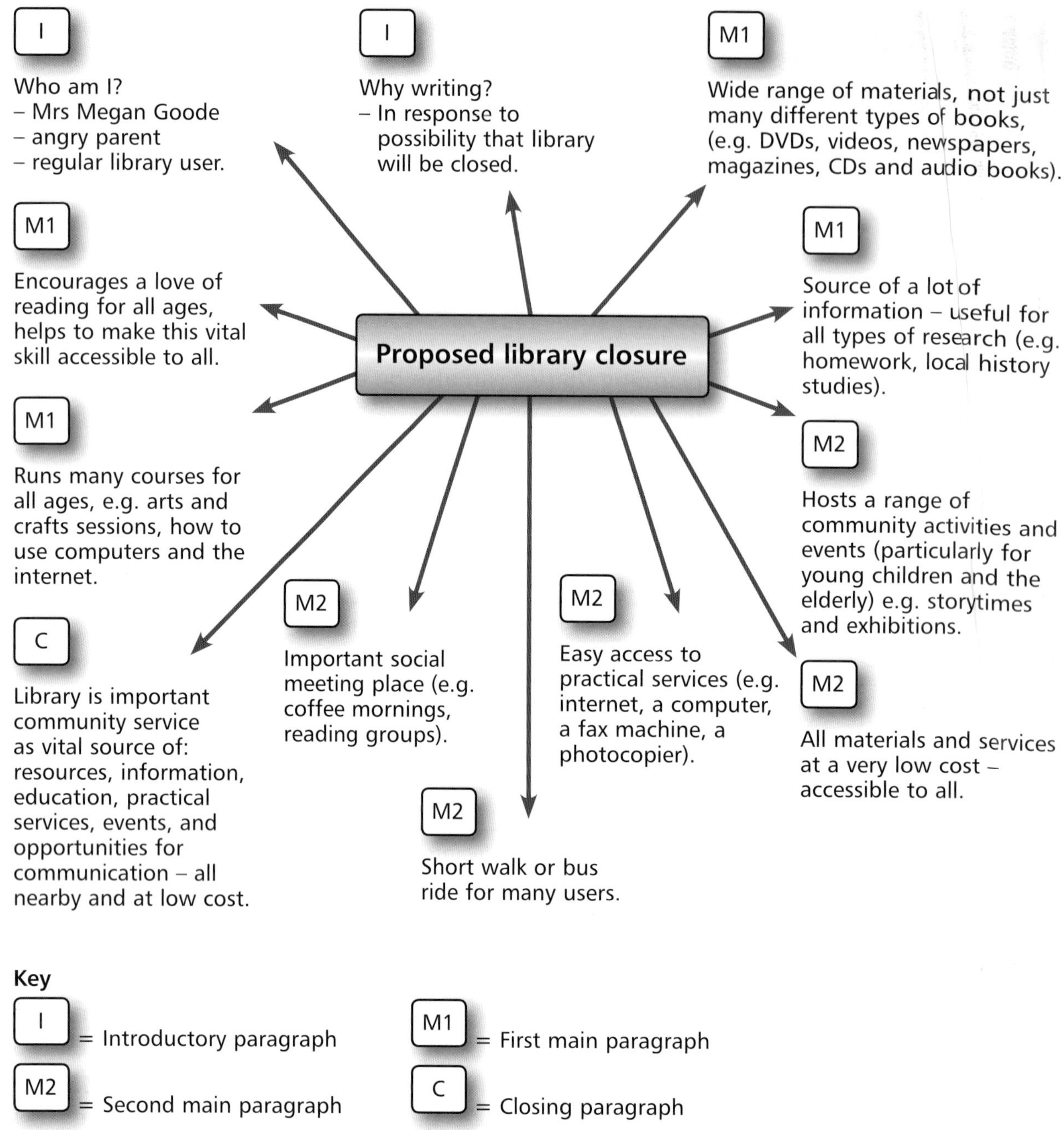

Key

I = Introductory paragraph	M1 = First main paragraph
M2 = Second main paragraph	C = Closing paragraph

- Formal sign-off =
  - Therefore, I hope you will investigate the issue of the proposed closure of our local library and I look forward to hearing from you shortly.
  - Yours faithfully [if Sir/Madam] or Yours sincerely [if making up name].
  - Signature.
  - Mrs Megan Goode (printed below).

The way in which you order your notes is likely to depend on the topic of the letter/ your reason for writing. For example, you may choose to order your points for a letter chronologically or in themes. In this example, the writer must show a range of reasons why the library should stay open, so it makes more sense to group similar ideas together into themed paragraphs rather than try to write them in a time sequence. Once grouped together, the points to be included within a paragraph should be arranged into a logical order so that they flow sensibly from one to the next.

Top Tip

Also see the section on recognising letter prompts (pages 13–14) for points on style and structure that you should have in mind when writing letters.

Now let's have a look at another letter prompt. In this example you could choose to order your points chronologically, according to what happened on each day of the week.

7 You have just received an exciting letter from your friend, Evie, telling you all about her summer holiday in Cornwall. Write a 350-word reply to her, describing what happened on your recent family holiday.

Your notes for this question might look like this:

- Writing to friend = informal letter
- Informal greeting style = Hi Evie! How's it going?

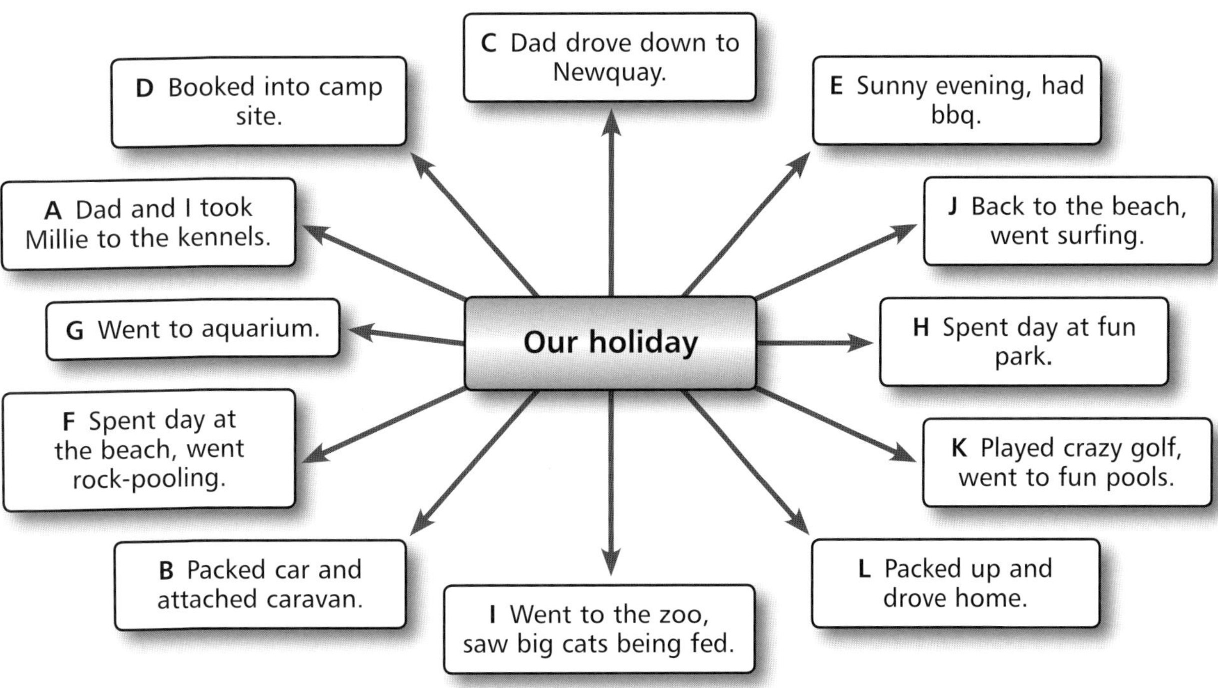

Key

A – E = Saturday
F = Sunday
I = Wednesday
J = Thursday

G = Monday
H = Tuesday
K = Friday
L = Saturday

- Informal sign-off =
  - Bye for now, write soon!
  - Love [your first name]

As you saw with diary entries, setting out your thoughts in a planning template can be an effective way of remembering particular rules about format and layout. As for diaries, both formal and informal letters also follow a series of rules relating to style and structure. As a result, you may find it helpful to note down your thoughts in a blank letter template, rather than a spider diagram. An example of a template for both styles of letter is given below.

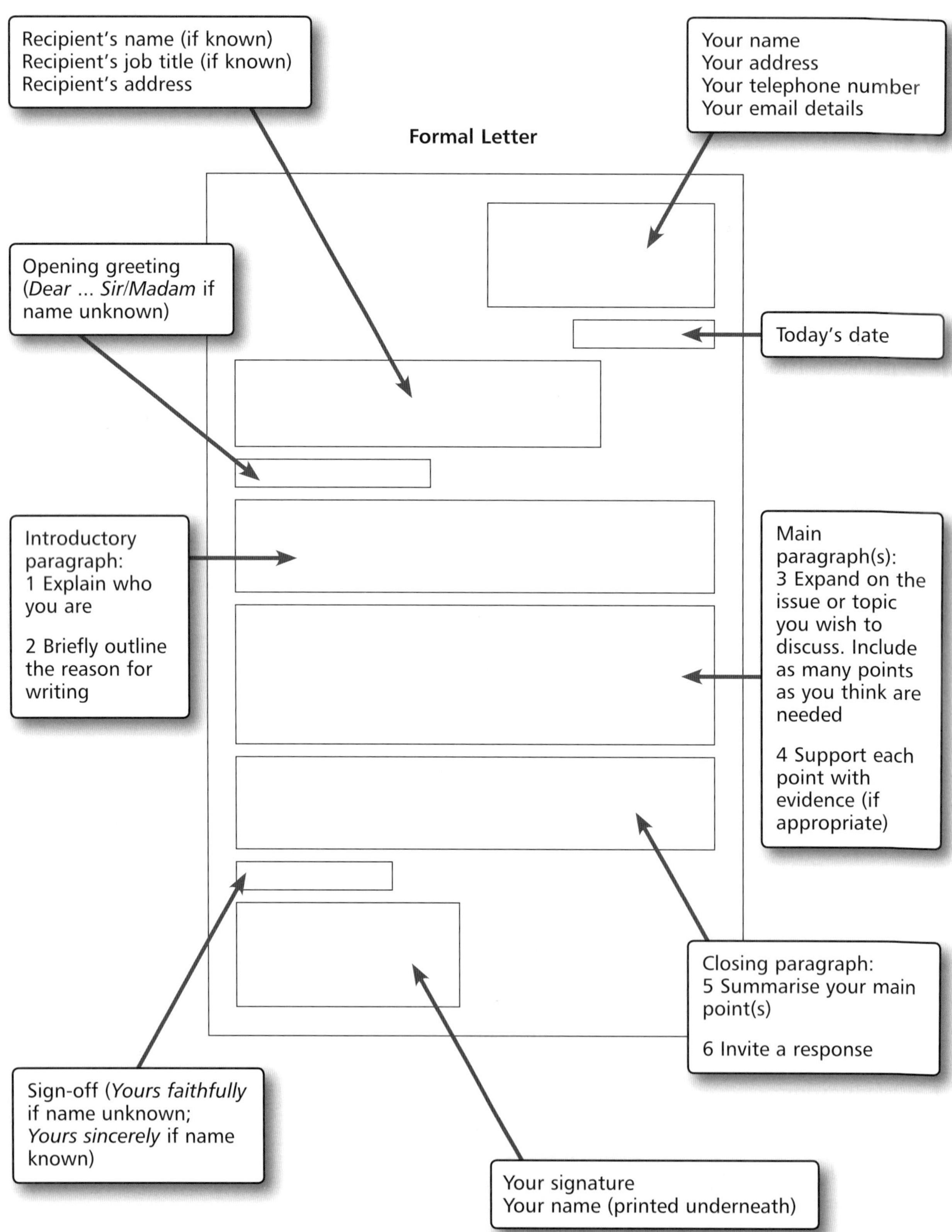

Informal Letter

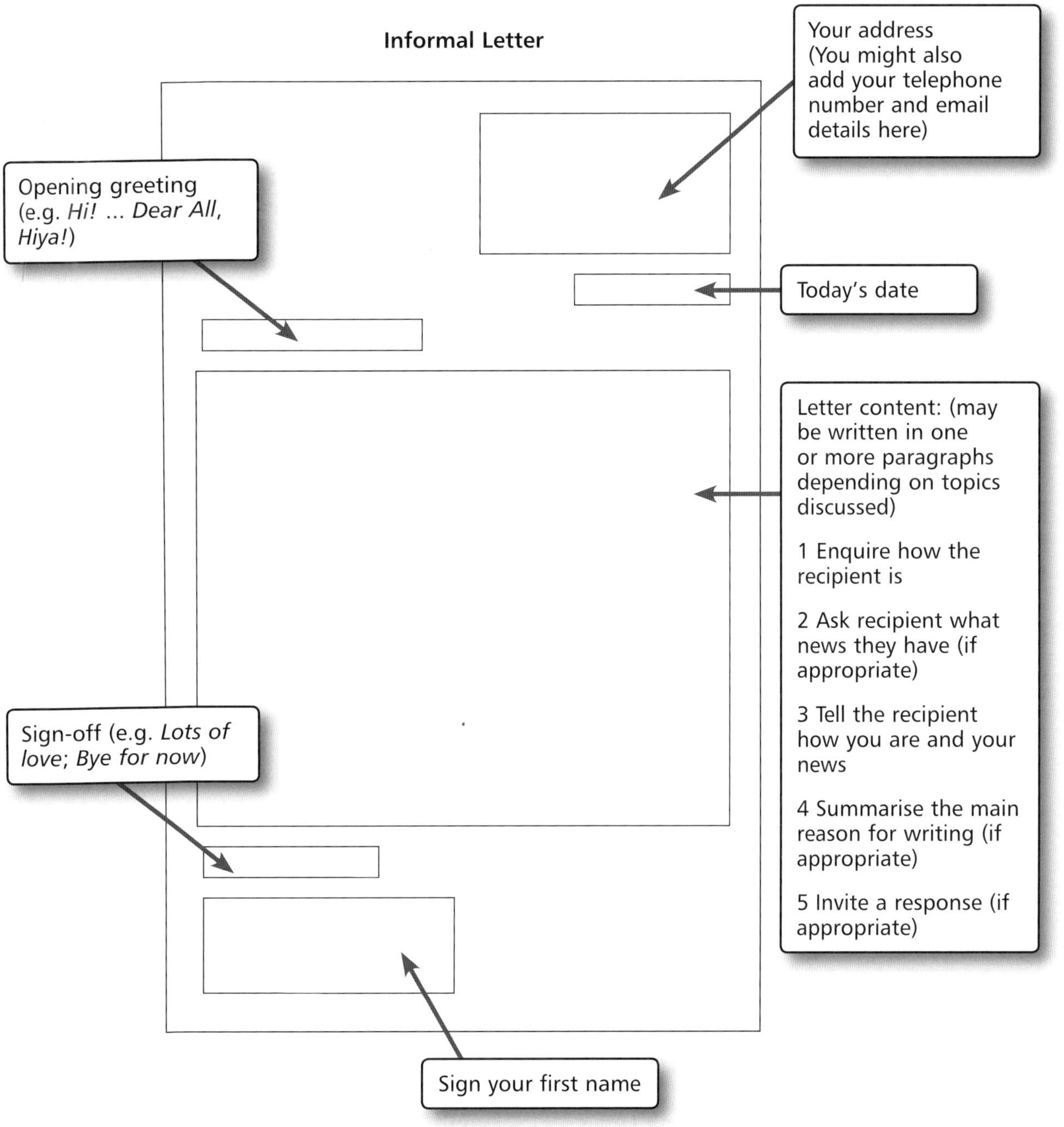

g *Planning a playscript*

You may have to continue a given scene from a play, create a scene out of a brief scenario or turn a piece of narrative into script form. However, no matter what style of playscript prompt you have to start from, you can follow the same planning process for your ideas.

1 First, quickly note down any hints you have been given about the plot, characters and setting.
2 Then, taking each of these aspects in turn, try to think of ways to expand them.
3 Next, think about how you will set the scene.
4 Then make brief notes on your opening.
5 Finally, note down your thoughts about your ending.

Top Tip

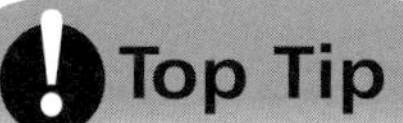

Kickstart your ideas by asking questions. The 'interrogate and interview' technique could be useful here.

Let's see how this might work for the following question prompt.

8 Best friends, Lewis and Callum, are in the playground at break. Callum is excited about his tenth birthday on Saturday, particularly because he is having a sleepover. However, Lewis has been told that he can't go to the party and so has to tell Callum that he won't be there. Explore and expand this scenario in the form of a playscript. Write up to one side of A4 paper. You do not need to finish the play.

So, following the plan outline above, you might choose to write your notes clearly in a grid like this:

What do I know about ...?	The plot	The characters	The setting
	• It is Callum's birthday on Saturday – he is having a sleepover. • Someone has told Lewis he can't go. • Lewis needs to tell Callum that he won't be there.	• Lewis – aged around 9–10 years. • Callum – aged 9, almost 10 years old. • Callum is excited. • The boys are best friends.	• School playground. • Break time. • Must be a weekday because the boys are at school.
How can I expand ...?	The plot	The characters	The setting
	• Who has told Lewis that he can't go? • How long has Lewis known that he won't be going? • Why can't Lewis go? Do his parents disapprove of sleepovers or is he going elsewhere? • Will this affect the boys' friendship? • Who else is going to the party? • What other fun activities are planned for the day?	• How does Lewis feel about not going to the party? • How will Callum feel when he knows that Lewis won't be there? • How long have they been friends? • How did they become friends?	• Exactly where are they in the playground? • Are the boys standing still or moving – maybe walking around or playing football? • What time is it? • Is it the start or end of break? • Is it a noisy area? • Who or what is near the boys? • What day is it? How long is it until the party on Saturday?

How to set the scene? Use a narrator or put hints about setting in dialogue?	Narrator could outline the playground setting before the boys speak: 'Meet Lewis and Callum, two nine-year-old boys who have been close friends since nursery school. Callum is the one in the red jumper racing around like a mad thing after the football; Lewis is the scrawny-looking one in goal. There's the bell; five minutes until the end of break. The game is over so Lewis walks over to meet Callum at the side of the pitch. We join their conversation just after he has announced that he won't be going to Callum's tenth birthday party.'
Ideas for opening? Grab the audience's attention straightaway or lead up to the climax?	Open with the boys in the middle of an argument or Callum at first thinking that Lewis is joking? Opening line: Callum (shocked): What do you mean that you're not coming? This is my big day!
Ideas for ending? Find a resolution or leave a cliff-hanger, leading to next scene?	Cliff-hanger – no resolution. Final lines: Lewis (nervously): We're still friends aren't we? Narrator: Lewis watches Callum walk off to the classroom with Sean. Lewis is alone.

Writing your ideas out like this should ensure that you remain focused on the question, while also helping you to create the basic structure of your scene. However, if you find it difficult to remember the key features of a playscript layout (such as how to write dialogue or stage directions), then you might prefer to make a different type of planning template. Here is a blank example of a different style that you might find useful:

Title:	Character list (and brief description of appearance, personality and so on): • • •
Setting the scene (use narrator?):	
Dialogue for scene – character name followed by : in the margin; new line per character	

	:	
	:	
	:	
	:	
	:	

	:	
	:	
	:	
	:	
	:	
	:	
	:	

Remember: **Plot** is told through dialogue – no speech marks – no direct speech verbs, e.g. 'said' – no descriptive passages.	Remember: **Stage directions** (written in brackets) are vital for: – highlighting character voices, actions, movements, appearances – setting the scene and atmosphere (props, lighting, sound effects).	Remember: **Punctuation** is needed throughout dialogue, for example: – full-stops – question marks – exclamation marks – dashes.

However you choose to make notes, when planning the actual dialogue for your scene try to remember these key points:

- *Include a mixture of dialogue lengths – several lines of one or two word comments can be difficult for an audience to follow, as can a lengthy speech by one character that goes on for pages and pages.*
- *Make sure that your dialogue and stage directions match logically – an audience will be confused by a character storming off if their dialogue is happy and light-hearted.*
- *Show your characters' personalities through realistic dialogue and behaviour. If you have decided that a character will be bossy and forceful, he is unlikely to stand silently and watch events unfold around him.*

If you are struggling to develop the plot in your plan then try thinking about the dialogue as a set of dominoes arranged vertically in a line. When the first one is pushed over it starts a chain reaction, with each domino knocking down the next one. The same effect can be seen in dialogue; a plot is developed through each character's response to what someone else has said.

A character can either feel and think or respond and react, creating a circle like this:

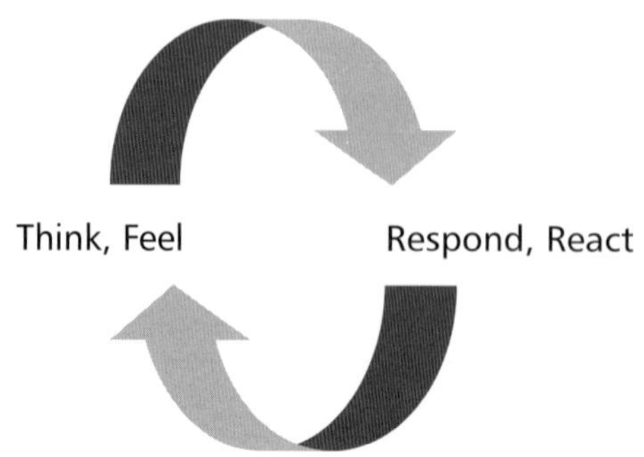

So, in the scene on page 74, Callum might feel angry, confused, hurt, disappointed or surprised that Lewis has said he cannot go to his party. Each of these feelings might provoke a different response and reaction from Callum. In turn, Callum's response will spark off particular thoughts and feelings for Lewis, which will impact on his response and so on.

Picturing the circle above as you plan your script should help you to write effective dialogue and to develop the plot logically. Always remember to keep the context of the question prompt in mind, though, as it can be easy to drift away from the task at hand!

(h) Planning a text continuation

The thought process behind planning this style of question can be different to other prompt types, due to the fact that your writing will continue from a given starting point (usually a few sentences, a short paragraph or a longer piece of comprehension text). Whatever the context of the given text, you must ensure that your writing not only continues straight on from where the extract finishes but that it follows a sensible path in line with the given text.

To help you structure your thoughts and plan your continuation, try following the TEMPO technique.

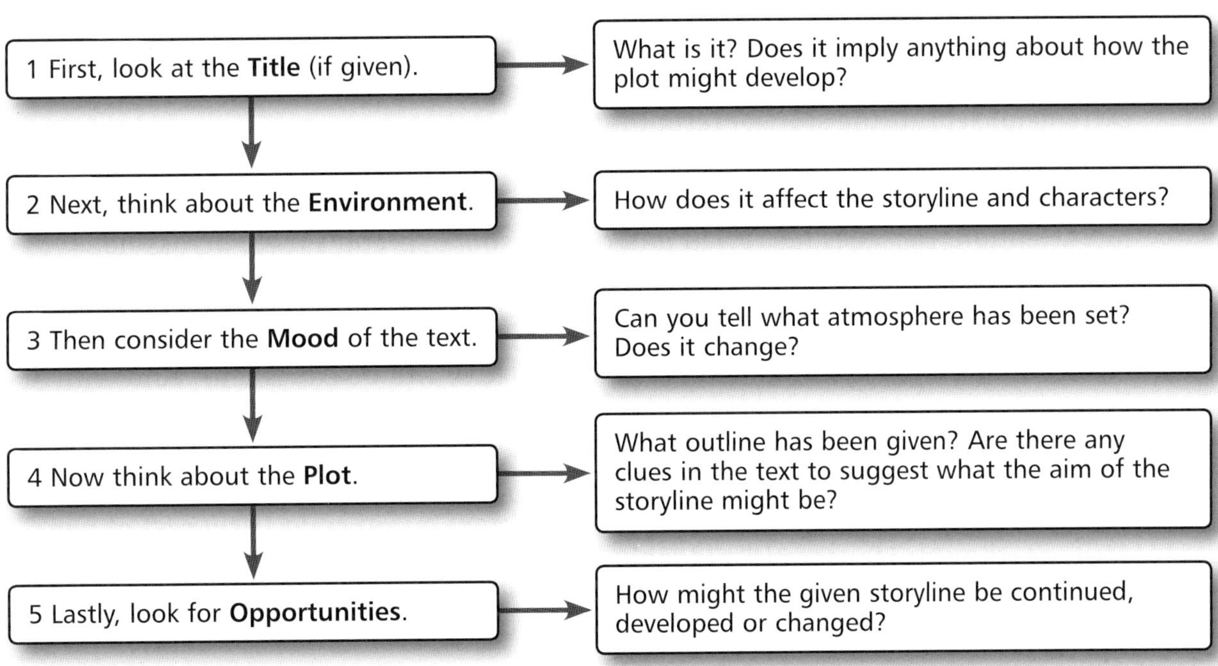

Let's see how this method might work. Here is an example text continuation prompt:

9 Read the following extract and then write the next stage in the story. Continue the passage in the same style and write no more than 400 words.

The downfall of Mrs Deville

Arabella and Charlotte held hands tightly and shuffled closer together. Their palms began to sweat and their knees shook. Right about now, the idea of smuggling the mobile phone in to school didn't seem such a good one. Charlotte reluctantly bent down, picked the phone up off the floor and handed the
5 offending object to Mrs Deville, their new Headteacher. The girls looked at each other; each knowing what the other was thinking – within minutes, their plan could be discovered!

"Who does this vile object belong to?" boomed Mrs Deville, the ends of her mouth twisting like an angry snake. All of the children and teachers stopped in
10 their tracks and turned to face the Head. An eerie silence fell over the corridor, everyone, including the teachers, too nervous to say anything. "If the guilty party does not have the courage to own up, then perhaps someone else is prepared to tell me who brought this contraband item on to school premises?" Again, silence descended over the crowd. "I see. I thought I had made it
15 extremely clear at the start of term that I shall not tolerate *any* of these toys or luxuries in *my* school? Apparently, I wasn't clear enough!"

Relishing the moment, the Head paused to make sure that she had everyone's full attention. Her eyes narrowed and an evil smirk spread slowly across her face as she announced, "Well, until the offender decides to admit their guilt, or
20 someone else chooses to give me their name, there will be severe penalties for all. Morning and afternoon breaks will be shortened by 10 minutes, everyone's lunch rations will be halved and all weekend leave will be cancelled!" And with that, she turned on her heel triumphantly and started to march off down the bleak corridor towards her cold, uninviting office.

25 A wave of low muttering erupted from the sea of shocked faces and Arabella began to panic. The ex-Sergeant Major was almost out of sight. Using all of her courage, the shy 10-year-old suddenly blurted out, "Mrs Deville, wait!" and then immediately wished that she hadn't. Mrs Deville stopped dead, spun round and fixed her frosty, unforgiving eyes firmly on Arabella …

Using the TEMPO technique, you might write out your notes for this question as follows:

Title?
- 'The downfall of Mrs Deville'.
- It sounds as if something unpleasant is going to happen to Mrs Deville.
- 'Deville' sounds similar to 'devil' – an indicator of her personality?

Environment?
- Set in a school corridor.
- Possibly a boarding school as the text refers to 'weekend leave'.
- The Head has set a strict regime that affects the children and the teachers.
- Corridor referred to as 'bleak', Head's office described as 'cold', 'uninviting' – sense of harsh surroundings fits the strict image of the Head.

Opportunities?
- The text ends with the Head staring at Arabella, waiting for her to speak.
- Where could the plot go from here?
  - Do Arabella and Charlotte own up and risk the Head's punishment?
  - Does Arabella name Charlotte or someone else as the culprit?
  - Does one of the teachers in the corridor step in to the conversation and stand up to the Head?
  - Do the girls manage to talk the Head round and get the phone back? If so, do they continue with their plan? What do they want the phone for?

Mood?
- Starts with a sense of fear (the girls standing close together, their hands sweating).
- The Head adds anger to the scene (she is like an 'angry snake').
- A nervous silence falls over the corridor (everyone is afraid of the Head).
- The Head shows a 'warped' sense of enjoyment and achievement from spreading fear – possibly because she used to be in the army?
- Shock travels through the crowd.
- Arabella panics.

TEMPO

Plot?
- Main characters: Arabella, Charlotte, Mrs Deville.
- Plot: The girls have smuggled in a mobile. Mrs Deville has found the phone and demands to know who has disobeyed school rules by bringing it on site. As no one owns up, she delivers some harsh punishments to everyone. Arabella calls to Mrs Deville as she walks away, causing the Head to stop and turn round. We are left wondering what Arabella will say and what Mrs Deville's reaction will be.
- Aim: to watch how the downfall of the evil Headteacher, Mrs Deville, unfolds.

Jotting down a few notes about the title, environment, mood and plot in a diagram like this will act as a reminder about what has happened so far. It should also help to ensure that your ideas (opportunities) for continuing the text make sense in the given context, as well as helping you to draw out some aspects from the text that you can then use in your own writing. Using the notes above, for example, you may choose to: directly refer to the school as a boarding school, include some more 'bleak' environment imagery, continue the sense of fear felt by the girls, include more details about the Head's army background and so on.

Remember: Title, Environment, Mood, Plot, Opportunities.

When writing in the style of someone else, underline words or phrases in the given text that you think you can reuse. Including these terms will help your continuation to follow the existing style. In this example, highlighting keywords such as 'shuffled', 'offending object', 'boomed', 'angry snake' and 'evil smirk' might lead you to write phrases such as:
– "Please stop *shuffling*, you're making me more nervous!" whispered Charlotte.
– Mrs Deville approached quickly, the *offending item* still in her hand.
– Arabella prepared herself for the Head's *booming* tones.
– The *snarling snake* flashed across Mrs Deville's face, making Arabella tighten her grip on Charlotte's hand.
– The Headteacher's *smirking* face was inches away from Arabella's.

(i) *Planning for a visual stimulus*

As for a text continuation, the process for planning a response to a visual stimulus prompt can be different from most other types of writing. This is because you will have been given a pictorial starting point for reference, but the question might require you to use the image to write in any one of a range of styles (a description, a fictional narrative, a debate, a text continuation or a style of your own choice, for example).

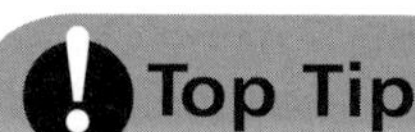

Look back at the relevant sections to remind yourself of the planning techniques for these different writing styles.

However, no matter what writing context you are given or what the visual aid shows, the following simple planning process can help you to tackle any style of visual prompt question.

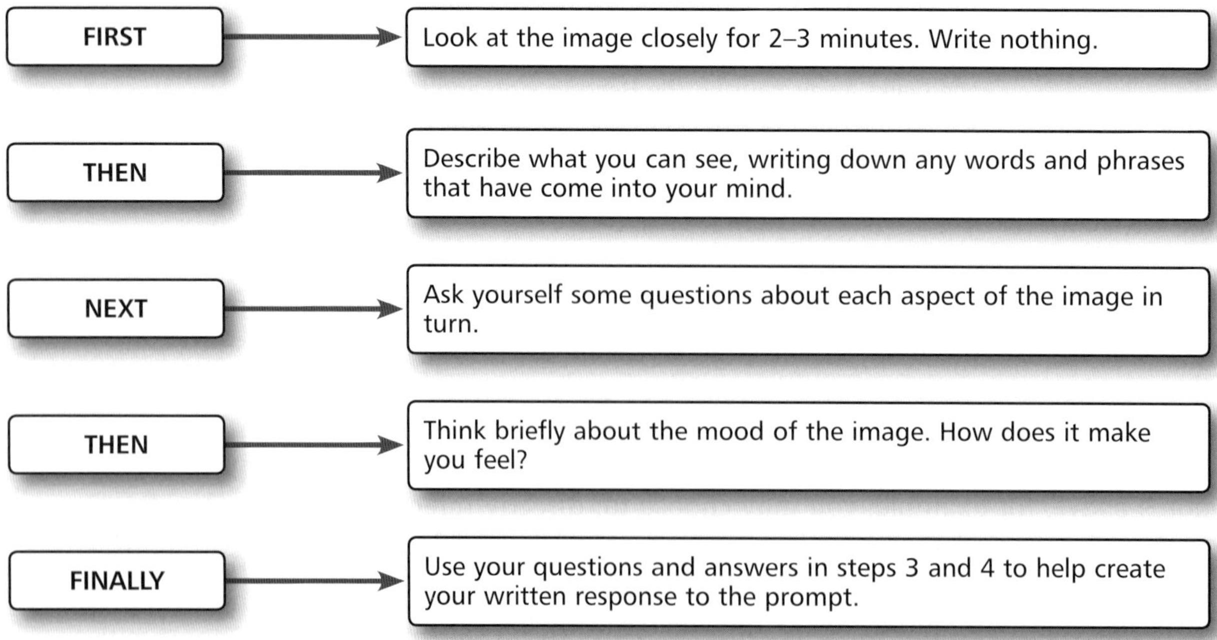

When you get to steps 2 and 3 of the above plan, imagine that you have to describe everything that you are looking at to someone who cannot see the image. This will help to make sure that your notes are as detailed as possible. Also, when you move on to step 3, try to consider each of the elements that you have noticed one at a time. This is important as it will not only ensure that you don't miss anything out but it will also encourage you to think logically about the image in front of you.

Here is a visual stimulus, with a range of question prompts that might accompany it.

Some writing prompts will invite you to write about a visual aid in any way that you wish. For this style of question, try to think about a range of possible themes that could relate to the image during step 1 of the plan. Then make a note of them during your brainstorming session in step 2. This should help you to generate some ideas that could form the basis of your writing.

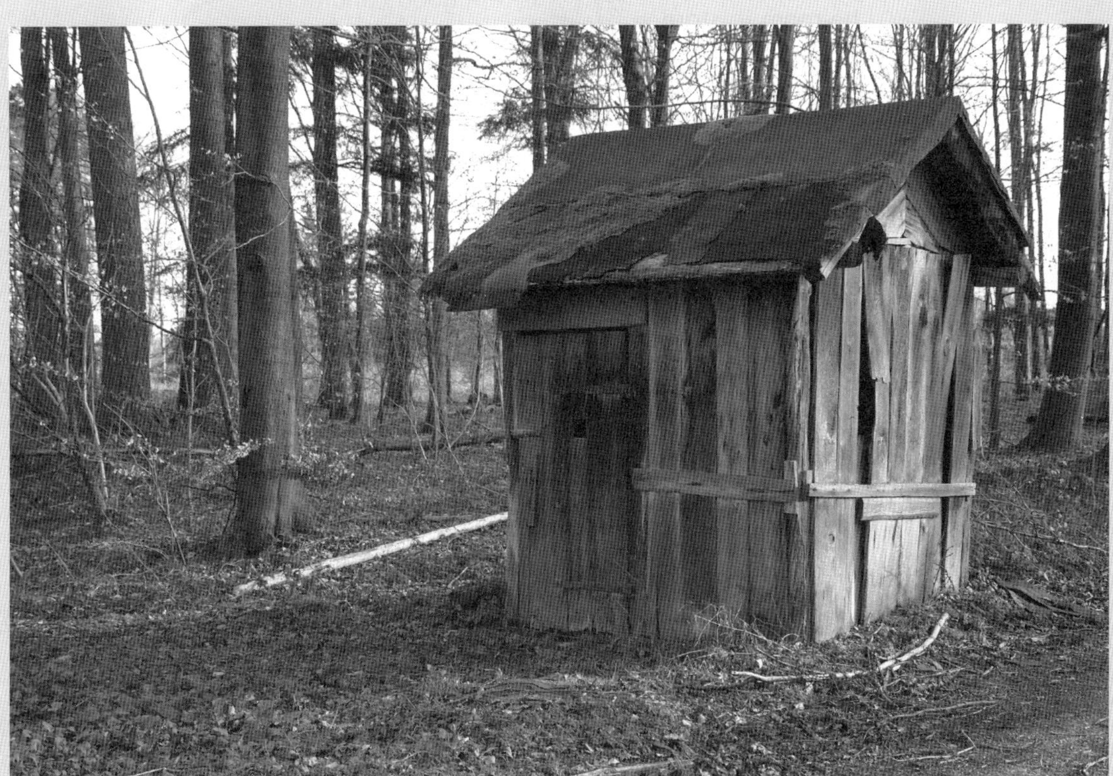

10 Look at this image. Write the opening section of a narrative entitled 'The Fox'. You should write no more that 400 words and you do not have to complete the story.

11 Discuss the following statement: The local forest is to be cut down. Refer to the given image in your answer. You may write up to one side of A4 paper.

12 Write a 300-word description of this picture.

13 Create a piece of writing, using this image in any way you wish.

Write 350–400 words.

14 Explain how this image makes you feel in 300 words.

So, having spent a few minutes looking at this image, you might choose to write down any ideas generated during steps 2 and 3 in a mind map:

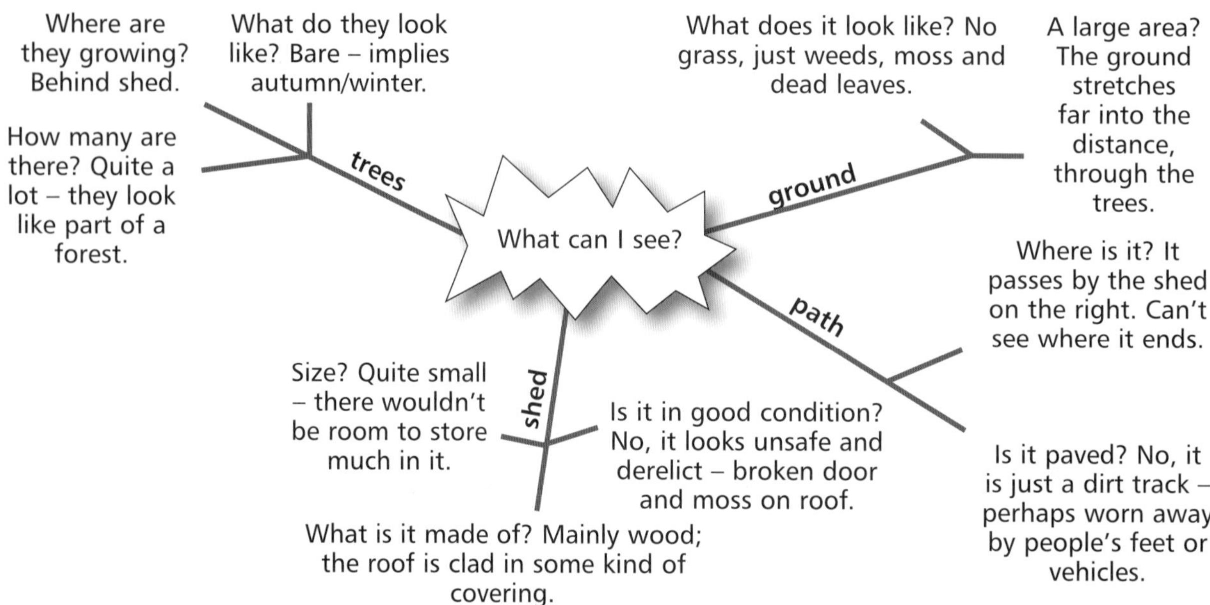

When you have written down all of your notes, it might be easier than you think to decide how an image makes you feel. For instance, in this example:

- *The bareness of the trees implies that it might be autumn or winter – these seasons might make you feel sad or cold.*
- *The shed looks unsafe and derelict – this might create a feeling of sadness and emptiness or of anticipation and excitement about what might be hidden inside.*
- *The shed is in the middle of a wood – this might make you wonder why it is there, what it used for and who uses it.*
- *Only a small part of the path is visible – this might make you wonder where it would lead if you were to follow it.*

Armed with all of your questions and answers about an image, as well as your knowledge of how to plan and write different text types, you should find it much easier to construct an answer to any given visual stimulus prompt.

(*j*) Planning a review

Reviews can be thought of as a mix of report and debate writing. As a result, a combination of the 4-step plans we looked at for these writing prompts can be useful for this style of writing.

 **Top Tip**

Remember to actively ask questions about an image. This will help get your ideas flowing quickly – much better than waiting for inspiration to come to you!

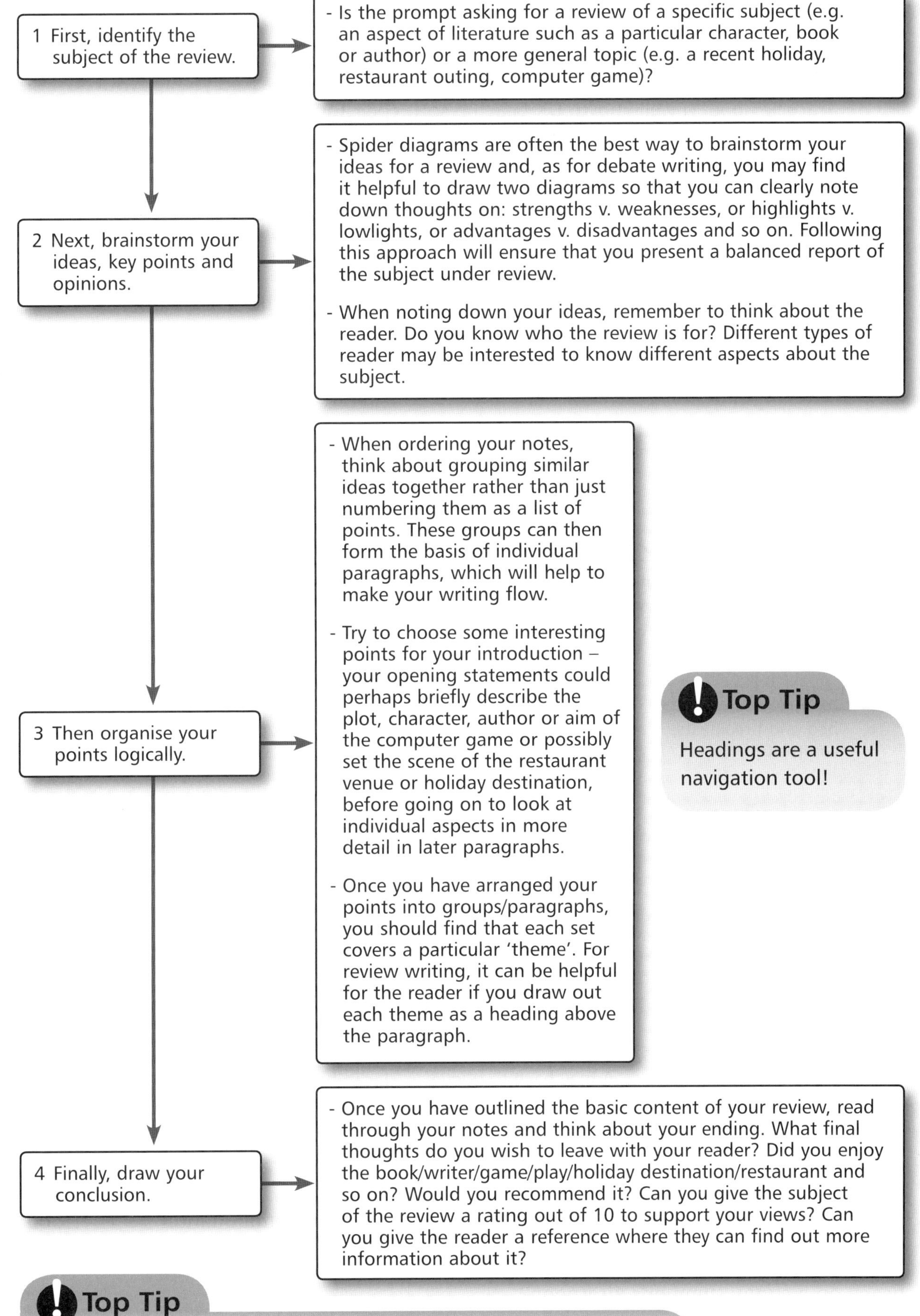

1 First, identify the subject of the review.

- Is the prompt asking for a review of a specific subject (e.g. an aspect of literature such as a particular character, book or author) or a more general topic (e.g. a recent holiday, restaurant outing, computer game)?

2 Next, brainstorm your ideas, key points and opinions.

- Spider diagrams are often the best way to brainstorm your ideas for a review and, as for debate writing, you may find it helpful to draw two diagrams so that you can clearly note down thoughts on: strengths v. weaknesses, or highlights v. lowlights, or advantages v. disadvantages and so on. Following this approach will ensure that you present a balanced report of the subject under review.

- When noting down your ideas, remember to think about the reader. Do you know who the review is for? Different types of reader may be interested to know different aspects about the subject.

3 Then organise your points logically.

- When ordering your notes, think about grouping similar ideas together rather than just numbering them as a list of points. These groups can then form the basis of individual paragraphs, which will help to make your writing flow.

- Try to choose some interesting points for your introduction – your opening statements could perhaps briefly describe the plot, character, author or aim of the computer game or possibly set the scene of the restaurant venue or holiday destination, before going on to look at individual aspects in more detail in later paragraphs.

- Once you have arranged your points into groups/paragraphs, you should find that each set covers a particular 'theme'. For review writing, it can be helpful for the reader if you draw out each theme as a heading above the paragraph.

Top Tip

Headings are a useful navigation tool!

4 Finally, draw your conclusion.

- Once you have outlined the basic content of your review, read through your notes and think about your ending. What final thoughts do you wish to leave with your reader? Did you enjoy the book/writer/game/play/holiday destination/restaurant and so on? Would you recommend it? Can you give the subject of the review a rating out of 10 to support your views? Can you give the reader a reference where they can find out more information about it?

Top Tip

Remember that a review can be based on real or imaginary events, so don't worry if you have no experience of the review asked for.

Let's see how this might work with a typical review question:

15 Happyholidays.co.uk, a new internet travel magazine, has asked you to write an article about a well-known UK beach resort. Their subscribers are mainly parents with young children. Your review should be no more than 400 words.

Following the planning process outlined above, your notes for this question might develop like this:

1   General topic – UK beach holiday destination, what does the seaside offer?

2–3 Readers: families with young children = will want to know about activities, accommodation, food outlets, etc.

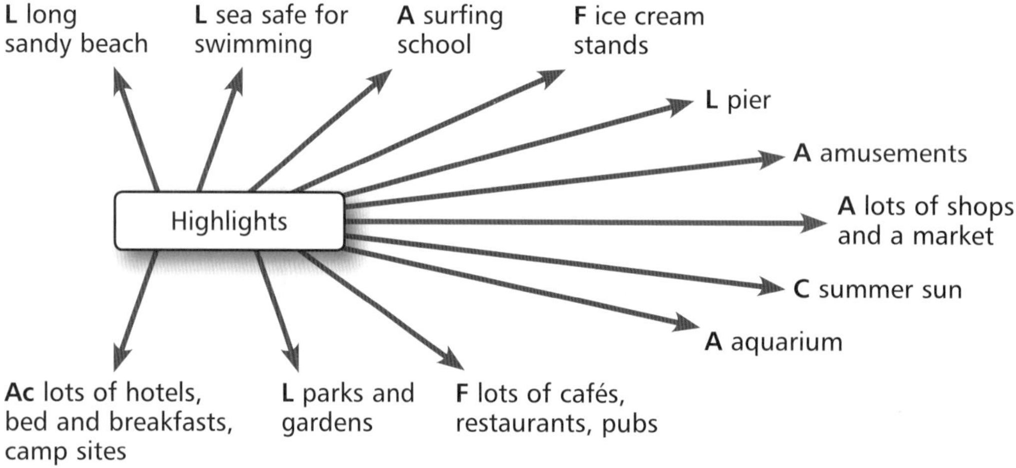

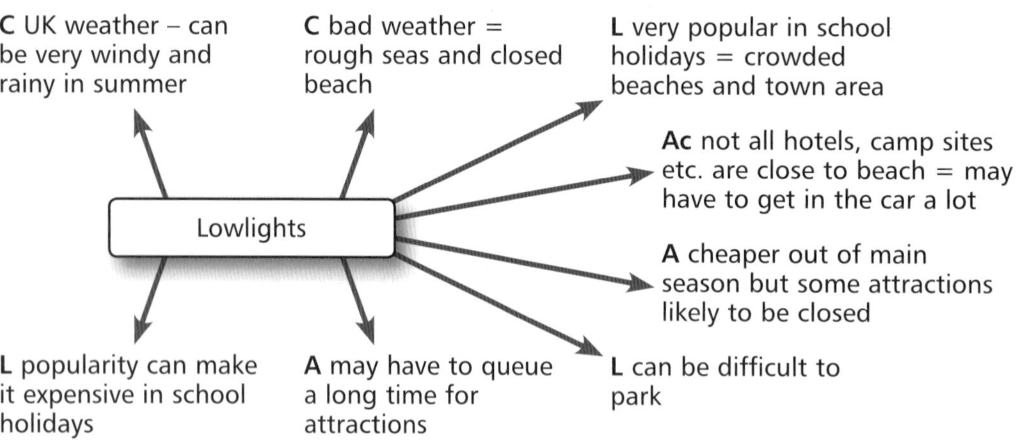

Key for paragraph themes – could form section headings

L = location   **C** = climate   **A** = attractions   **Ac** = accommodation   **F** = food

Notes on introduction – draw reader in by describing a family picnic/day out on the beach on a sunny summer's afternoon?

4 Final thoughts – highly recommended for family holiday; something for everyone; book early to get cheaper deals; plan some indoor activities for bad weather days; for more information, visit the local tourism website.

Following this style of plan should enable you to structure your thoughts clearly and make sure that you group similar ideas together. This will help to ensure that the flow of your writing is logical and that your reader will easily be able to navigate through the review.

However, if you don't want to organise your review ideas using spider diagrams, then here is another technique you might like to try. It involves imagining that you are walking down a set of steps, working your way inwards from the outside of your review topic. Here's how this method could work for any restaurant review.

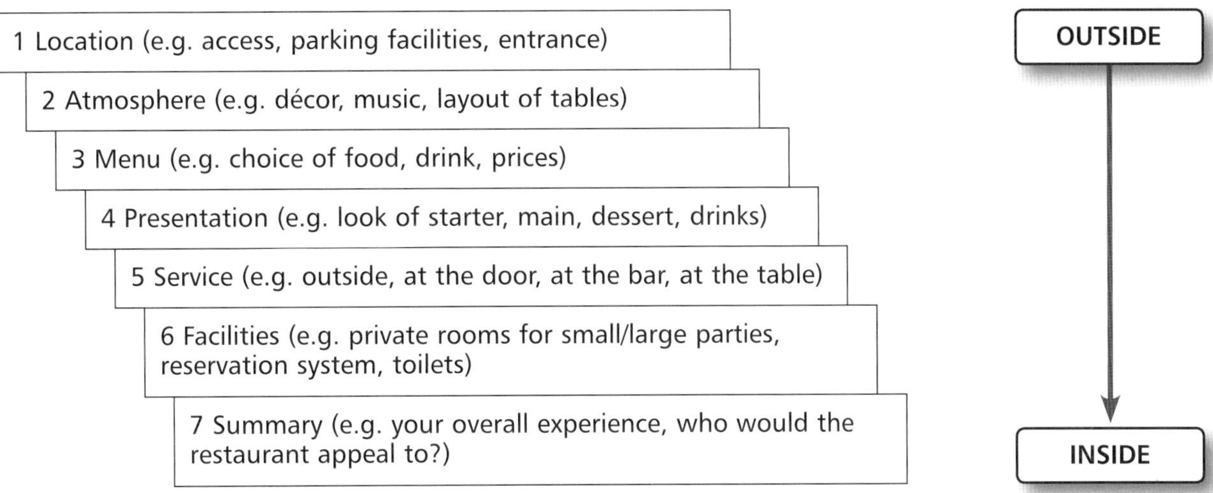

And here's an example of how you might use it for a book review:

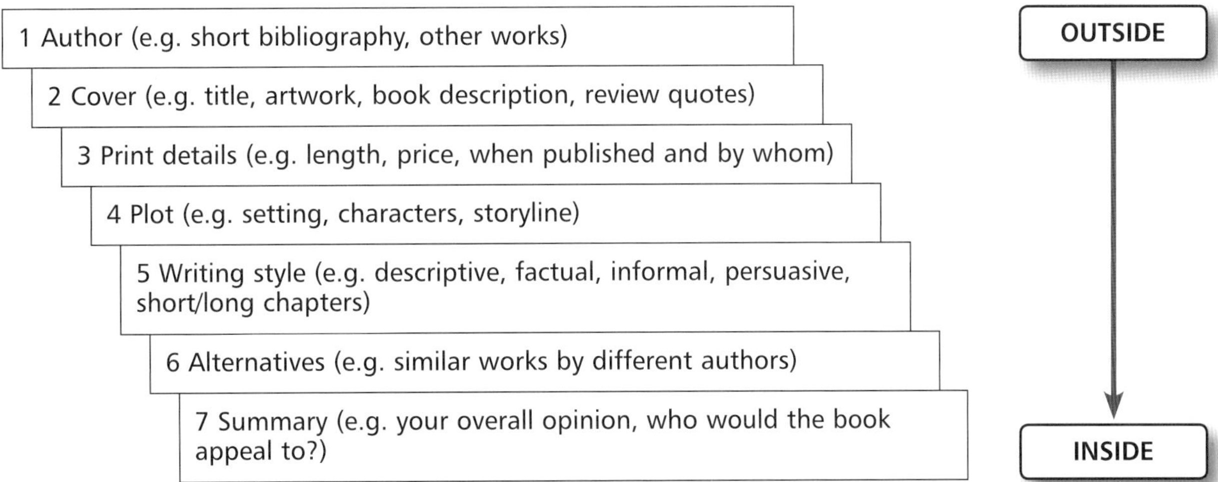

Each of these examples has seven steps but you could add more or fewer steps depending on your topic. Think of each step as a theme, a heading or the subject of a paragraph. Like the key shown in the earlier spider diagrams, these steps will help you to collate your similar ideas together and provide a clear structure for your review.

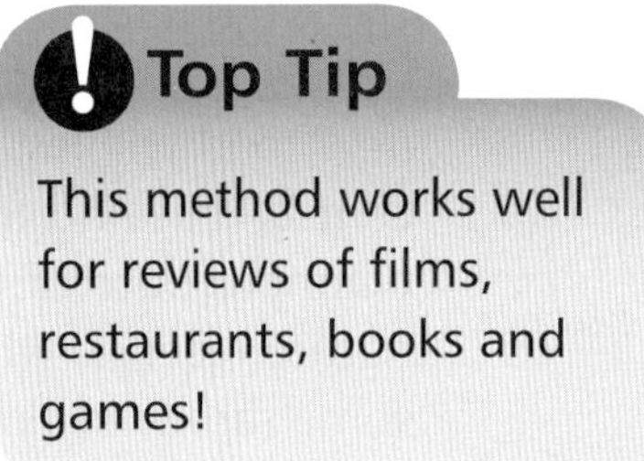
Top Tip

This method works well for reviews of films, restaurants, books and games!

A plan is a tool that will help you to organise your thoughts for any question type but don't let your plans restrict your writing. Remember that you can alter, add or expand ideas as you go along and that the planned order of points or events might also need to change as you develop your response. Try to think of any plan that you create as a place to:

Top Tip

An examiner might give you some marks for the plan itself as this is your 'working out', so try to make all of your plans clear and easy to follow just in case!

- *note down what the question is asking you to do*
- *brainstorm all of your thoughts and ideas*
- *organise your notes into a logical order for writing.*

Once you have a good plan, writing up your answer should be much faster and easier to do.

Now it's your turn!

Prepare a plan for each of the following writing prompts. Once you have completed each plan, check back through the advice and strategies given in the relevant section to remind yourself of the key points for each type.

16 Discuss the following question: Should mobile phones be banned in schools? Write up to one side of A4 paper.

17 Write a 350-word report about the events at your local school's summer fête.

18 Describe your favourite activity in 300–350 words.

19 Use the picture on the right as a basis for any piece of writing. Write no more than 400 words.

20 Write a piece of creative writing entitled 'The Magic Box'. You should write no more than 400 words.

21 You and a friend have just completed an all-day treasure hunt. To make sure that you don't forget anything that's happened, you decide to write today's entry in your diary straight away. Record the day's events in 300–350 words.

22 You have just learned that a new ring road has been proposed in your area. The new road will lessen the amount of traffic that has to pass through the town centre, relieving the traffic congestion at peak times of the day. However, the planned route of the road will mean that it will run parallel to a well-established nature reserve, which is home to many species of animals and birds as well as some rare wild flowers. Write to your local council expressing your views on the proposed site of the road. Write up to 300 words.

23 Read the following extract and then continue the text in the given style. Write up to 400 words.

Corinne could hardly believe what was in front of her. She slowly shut her tired eyes, counted to 10 and then opened them again. They were still there. In the newly-fallen snow she could clearly see minute hoof marks – marks that were far too small to have been made by horses or Farmer Jo's cows.

5 Panic started to set in. What on earth had come into her garden?

With her eyes firmly fixed on the mysterious indentations, Corinne followed them down to the end of the path. When she reached the gate, the trail went cold. In the hope of catching sight of the creator of these dimples, she leant out over the garden wall and looked up and down the street. Everywhere

10 was silent. It was still very early; the rest of the village was fast asleep. At that moment, standing there shivering in her nightdress, she felt like she was the only person on earth.

Fresh feathery flakes began drifting drowsily down from the off-white blanket above her. Another heavy snowfall was coming and the thought of

15 it made her shiver again. "Time to get indoors," Corinne surmised, so she turned and took a few steps back up the path towards the house. As she did so, she heard a faint snuffling noise coming from the other side of the wall. She retraced her steps as quickly and as quietly as she could and peered cautiously over the gate ....

24 You have been asked to write a 350-word review of the new High Street store that has just opened. Your article will be printed in the weekend edition of your local newspaper. The Editor is particularly keen to read details about:

- the store's owner and reasons behind them opening the shop in that location
- the range of products on offer
- whether the goods appear to offer value for money
- who is most likely to want to shop there
- anything else you think would be of interest to the reader.

25 Finish this scene in no more than 450 words.

Narrator: School finished over an hour ago. Paul and Deepak have been waiting for the last teacher to leave so that they can come out of hiding and go on the hunt. Their pulses begin to race as they hear the caretaker's advancing footsteps. The door rattles and, satisfied that the office is locked, he moves on down the corridor. With that, the boys emerge.

Paul: See, I told you it would be easy. Now, where's the torch?

Deepak: Are you sure this is a good idea? It seemed a great plan this morning but now ...

Paul: Don't be a chicken. How cool will it be tomorrow when we show everyone the photo of 'Moaning Minnie'? That'll show George that she exists!

Now discuss your plans with someone else. Does each one give a clear structure that could form the basis of a relevant written response? Can either of you think of any ways in which you could improve your plans?

⬤ Develop language skills

By this stage you should have learnt some key ways for generating ideas if you get stuck, know how best to plan a response and feel ready to start writing. However, before you set off, take a moment to think about whether the type of vocabulary you are going to use is really appropriate for the task. Also, consider whether your chosen language style will present your writing skills in the best way. Have you thought enough about how you will create interest, emotion and variety in your writing? This is where language skills are vital and this section will show you how to use vocabulary and layout to improve your writing.

Whether you are composing a letter, recount, debate, playscript or piece of narrative, for example, your writing should offer the reader sufficient depth and substance to enable them to engage with the text. One way to tackle this process is to think about a skeleton. A skeleton is the core of a person's body which is built up through encasing the bones in layers of muscle and skin. In the same way, the basic facts (or bare bones) of a piece of writing can be 'fleshed out' through using different writing techniques to add details.

So how can you make your writing interesting enough so that it comes to life and engages the reader? Here are some top tips. Note them down and then practise the range of related exercises and techniques that are explored in the following sections.

- *Use different length sentences.*
- *Include monosyllabic and polysyllabic words.*
- *Apply a wide vocabulary.*
- *Consider the strength of meaning.*
- *Introduce the senses.*
- *Create the right image.*

Let's have a look at each of these points in turn.

(a) Use different length sentences

Combining a range of sentence lengths throughout your writing will not only create a visual effect within a piece of text, but it will also help your writing to flow. Using different sentence lengths allows you to create variety and interest for your reader by perhaps building tension with shorter, sharper sentences and providing the contrast with longer, more flowing sentences. Additionally, using this writing technique will highlight your ability to use conjunctions and punctuation to connect phrases, clauses and sentences.

Look at paragraphs A and B below. They both describe the same event, but which one flows more easily as you read?

Extract A

It rained heavily last Tuesday. I was on my way to school. Fortunately I had my umbrella with me. Even with my umbrella my feet were wet. My friend Kayleigh was waiting for me at the school gate. I have known Kayleigh for three years now. We always wait for each other at the school gate. Our first lesson was English. English is my favourite lesson. We are working on extended writing. I really enjoy extended writing.

Extract B

It rained heavily last Tuesday while I was on my way to school. Fortunately I had my umbrella with me, but even with my umbrella my feet were wet. My friend Kayleigh, who I have known for three years now, was waiting for me. We always wait for each other at the school gate. Our first lesson was English – my favourite! We are working on extended writing, which I really enjoy.

Paragraph A should have felt quite monotonous to read, due to the fact that it consists of 11 short sentences that repeat some of the same information. Paragraph B provides the same amount of detail but it combines the information into six sentences that include a range of punctuation and connective words.

Top Tip

Read back through each paragraph as you write to check whether you can improve your writing. Could you combine sentences, introduce conjunctions or use punctuation (such as commas and dashes) to remove any unnecessary repetition?

Now it's your turn!

Read the following paragraph.

Wilson and Jason are two brothers. They live with their family in Liverpool. Both brothers love football. They both support Liverpool. They both love their computer games. Jason is older than Wilson. He is two years older than Wilson. Wilson is very good at maths. He enjoys maths. Jason is better at English. He enjoys English. Both boys enjoy Spanish. They both dislike French.

Now, through using a range of conjunctions and introducing appropriate punctuation, revise these sentences. Think about how the reading flow can be improved. Look out for repetition and remember that you can always take out or change words around to create a more interesting paragraph.

(b) Include monosyllabic and polysyllabic words

These terms may sound complicated but they just refer to the number of syllables in a word: monosyllabic (consisting of one syllable); polysyllabic (consisting of more than one syllable).

All words can be broken down into their syllables (stresses within a word such as but-ter-fly or ta-ble) and these syllables help to create a rhythmic reading flow in a piece of writing. The extracts below highlight the way in which syllables can affect a reader's experience.

Read the following extract. The number below each word shows the number of syllables
that it contains.

Extract A

The trains from the North all come and go from platform seven. There is so
1   1   1   1   1   1   1   1   1   1   2   2   1   1 1
much noise as people get on and off their trains. As my train pulls in I find my
1   1   1   2   1   1 1   1   1   1   1   1 1   1   1 1 1 1   1
seat. I am glad to see that I am by the window. I place my bag on the shelf and
1   1 1   1   1 1   1   1 1 1   1   2   1 1   1   1   1   1   1   1   1
get out my lunch.
1   1   1   1

In this extract, the sentences are mainly made up of monosyllabic words. In fact, the text
only contains four polysyllabic words (plat-form, sev-en, peo-ple, win-dow) which each
consist of two syllables. This overuse of monosyllabic words creates quite a 'choppy' and
'detached' effect when the text is read. As it is simple to read and contains quite basic
words, this style of text is ideal for a young reader. For anyone else, this monosyllabic
tone can quickly become quite monotonous and dull to read.

Let's have a look at another example:

Extract B

Every locomotive travelling Northwards announces its arrival and departure
3   4   3   2   3   1   3   1   3
from platform seven. There's a horrendous cacophony as numerous passengers
1   2   2   1   1   3   4   1   3   3
hurriedly embark and disembark locomotives. As my locomotive commences,
3   2   1   3   4   1 1   4   3
I locate my seating area. I'm very happy to observe that I'm comfortably
1 2   1   2   3   1   2   2   1   2   1   1   4
accommodated beside the window facing forwards. I position my suitcase upon
5   2   1   2   2   2   1   3   1   2   2
the overhead projection and unpack delicious homemade sandwiches.
1   3   3   1   2   3   2   3

Can you see how this extract reads differently to Extract A? This example has a greater
mix of monosyllabic and polysyllabic words, which creates a more rhythmic effect.
However, can you imagine reading a lengthy piece of writing that was all written in this
style? With its focus mostly on polysyllabic words (40, as opposed to 20 monosyllabic
ones) and heavy use of quite complex vocabulary, the reader would quickly find an
extended narrative of this nature quite dense and tiring.

Let's look at one more example:

Extract C

All locomotives travelling North arrive and depart from platform seven. There's
 1   4   3   1   2   1   2   1   2   2   1
a horrendous noise as numerous passengers hurriedly get on and off their
1   3   1 1   3   3   3   1 1 1 1 1
trains. As my train pulls in I locate my seat. I'm very happy to see that I'm
  1   1 1   1   1 11 2   1   1   1 2   2 1 1 1 1
sitting beside the window facing forwards. I place my suitcase on the overhead
   2   2   1   2   2   2 1 1   1   2   1 1   2
shelf and get out my delicious homemade sandwiches.
  1   1   1   1   1   3   2   3

How did you feel reading this version of the text? You should be able to see that Extract C has combined some of the words and phrases from both previous extracts, now containing 23 polysyllabic and 38 monosyllabic words. Introducing a lower number of polysyllabic words has still created a rhythmic effect for the reader but, unlike Extract B, it is no longer overwhelming to read. Instead, scattering the more complex vocabulary amongst the more basic, monosyllabic words helps to add interest while giving a comfortable reading flow to the piece.

Top Tip

Remember that syllables create rhythm and pace and that having a good mix of monosyllabic and polysyllabic words in your writing will help to generate atmosphere and also keep your reader engaged.

Now it's your turn! Place 40 of the garden-related words below under the correct headings in the grid. To help you get started, the first four words have been added.

~~rose, daisy, marigold, wisteria~~, weeds, honeysuckle, broom, daffodil, holly, conifer, loganberry, tulip, tomatoes, ladybird, sprouts, celeriac, pears, spade, crocus, grasses, escallonia, chrysanthemum, carrots, millipede, lettuces, asparagus, fork, hoe, parsnips, Rotavator, apples, ivy, wheelbarrow, shed, rhododendron, pond, mistletoe, geranium, pumpkin, lavender, cauliflower

1 syllable	2 syllables	3 syllables	4 syllables
rose	daisy	marigold	wisteria

(c) Apply a wide vocabulary

How do you choose the words you want to include in your writing? For example, do you write down the first words that come to mind when describing something or do you stop and think about the effect you want your words to create in the reader's mind? You can play around with words to create all sorts of images, patterns, rhythms and effects, but to do this successfully requires broad word knowledge.

So how can you expand your existing vocabulary? In this section, you'll learn how three simple writer's tools (a dictionary, a thesaurus and a notepad) can really help you to increase your word knowledge.

Keep a dictionary and a thesaurus close to hand

A dictionary and a thesaurus are two of the most vital tools that a successful writer can have because they hold a wealth of wonderful information. While a dictionary will provide you with details of word origins, spellings, pronunciations, meanings and examples of how each word can be used, a thesaurus enables you to find a word and choose from several alternatives (synonyms) that have the same or a similar meaning.

For example, checking the word 'nice' in a dictionary will confirm its spelling and explain that it means 'something pleasant, satisfactory and positive', while looking up 'nice' in a thesaurus will highlight many alternative words that can replace it in a range of different contexts, such as: good, agreeable, lovely, polite, fine, friendly, delightful, enjoyable and kind.

'Nice' is just one example of many overused words that we often include in our writing. If you really want to make your writing sparkle, spend some time thinking about the words you use regularly in your writing and try to note down some more interesting synonyms for them.

Here is a list of some other commonly used words to get you started. Look them up in a thesaurus and find a better replacement for each one:

and	*cold*	*happy*	*old*
bad	*fast*	*light*	*pretty*
because	*go*	*like*	*sad*
big	*good*	*little*	*say*

Remember that the wider your word knowledge, the more interesting, descriptive and colourful your writing will become for the reader. So, whenever you read or hear a word that you have not come across before, make sure that you look it up in a dictionary to find out what it means (it might have several different meanings in different contexts) and then check for alternatives in a thesaurus. For more help on synonyms and antonyms, see *Bond How to do ... 11⁺ English* section D9.

If you don't have a paper copy of your dictionary or thesaurus to hand, don't worry. Most word processing packages now have an in-built dictionary and thesaurus tool. If you highlight a word and then click the right-hand mouse button, an options menu should appear. One of these options should allow you to 'look up' the highlighted word either in a dictionary or thesaurus. Another option on the list may display a set of 'synonyms' straightaway for you to choose from.

Now it's your turn!

Replace each word in brackets with a different, more expressive synonym or phrase. If you get stuck, you can use your thesaurus for ideas, but remember to check that your alternatives make sense within the given context.

I (like)__________ art, history and geography but I am (bad) __________ at languages. I think my school is (good) __________ as we have some (nice) __________ teachers who make the lessons (good) __________ and our classroom resources are (good) __________. We have a (big) __________ hall and a (big) __________ playground.

Keep a small notepad in your pocket or bag

A pocket-sized notebook is another secret weapon that writers often use, as it ensures that no matter where they are they always have somewhere to record their thoughts. If you are determined to produce really effective writing, then try to carry a notepad and pencil or pen with you to make sure you can capture lots of ideas each day.

If you are wondering where all of these ideas might come from, then here are some top tips.

- *As you read any book, leaflet, poster, magazine or comic, be on the lookout for attention-grabbing words, phrases, captions, headlines or descriptive passages.*
- *Listen to conversations between your friends, family, neighbours and teachers or people on the bus, at school or in a shop. Are they using any interesting or unfamiliar dialect terms, forms of greeting, phrases and so on that could be useful when writing dialogue? Or try tuning the radio to a debate or an interview to hear the words people use to persuade, defend or criticise.*
- *As you watch your favourite television programme or see any adverts, keep your ears open for any appealing, exciting or unusual phrases!*
- *While you're out and about, or even sitting in the dentist's waiting room, look at the people around you. What are they wearing, how do they move, what are they doing? All of this input could be useful for character descriptions.*

If you follow these tips, you should soon build up a wide selection of key terms and phrases that you can then draw on for your own writing. Make sure, though, that you avoid including the names and addresses of 'real' people in your writing. Your Aunty Gladys who lives at number 1 Swan Road, Seisdon, for example, might not appreciate you suggesting that she is suffering with wind! Instead, browse the telephone book for a wide choice of surnames and try scanning a road atlas for place names.

Of course, you can use your notebook to record a wide range of information in many different ways. You might, for example, choose to collate essential key terms relating to particular topics in the form of checklists or mini dictionaries. This format can be especially useful for word groups such as colours, smells, food types, materials and lists of words showing different degrees of size, speed, hardness, heat and so on.

Here are a couple of examples:

A checklist of colours might begin like this.

COLOUR	SHADE
black	charcoal, tar, liquorice, carbon
blue	navy, sapphire, cobalt, indigo
brown	chocolate, coffee, mocha, tan, mushroom
burgundy	ruby, wine, mauve, plum, maroon
cream	beige, stone, buttermilk, almond, magnolia, natural

You might start a collection of descriptive terms for types of food as follows.

FOOD TYPE	DESCRIPTION
apple	rotten, crisp, crunchy, sour, juicy
banana	soft, mushy, sweet, bruised, over-ripe
cheese	dense, soft, creamy, sharp, tangy
chocolate	gooey, silky, milky, sweet, flaky
toast	dry, chewy, burnt, soggy, hard

Top Tip

Don't be scared to pinch other writers' ideas. The more you read, the more you are exposed to a variety of vocabulary, and if you find a phrase or word that you like, use it in your writing.

Top Tip

Don't forget to use a dictionary to look up any unfamiliar words that you hear or read. Remember to say the word, spell the word and write out the word so that you can recall it later.

Top Tip

Most DIY stores have free paint cards or booklets showing different colour ranges. Try to collect a few of these and stick them in your notebook, as they are a really useful resource for descriptions of colour shades.

Or you might like to use your notebook to revise and expand your knowledge of specific parts of speech, such as verbs, adverbs and adjectives. Here are some fun and memorable ways of recording details about these elements of language.

Top Tip

Remember to keep your thesaurus and dictionary with you. A thesaurus is an ideal source for synonyms and you can check the meaning of any unfamiliar words in a dictionary.

1 Expand your knowledge of verbs by choosing a common verb, such as 'walk', and creating a verb clock around it that shows up to 12 more descriptive synonyms for the verb in the centre.

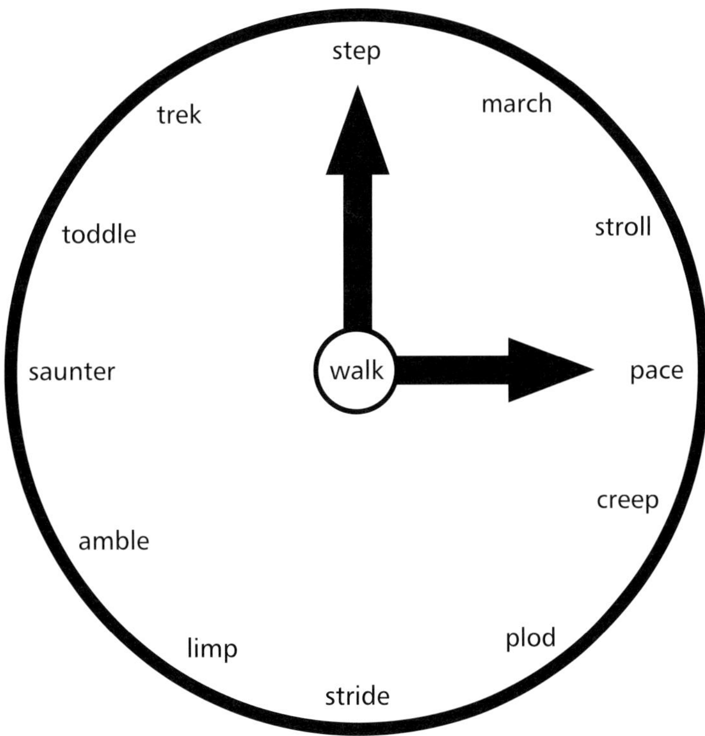

The 12 alternative verbs in this example all describe different ways of walking but, like the descriptions of colour shades in the checklist above, they each have their own associations. This means that through choosing your words and phrases carefully, you can control the reader's understanding of an event and the image created in their mind's eye.

Let's look at a few sample sentences based on some of the 'walking verbs':

The girl *ambled* back to her Mum.   implies: She was unhurried.
The girl *strode* back to her Mum.   implies: She was confident or annoyed.
The girl *trekked* back to her Mum.   implies: She was far away.
The girl *toddled* back to her Mum.   implies: She was young.

You can see that each verb suggests a very different image or mood in these sentences, so it is important to consider the impression that you want your words to create. You can also weaken your writing or confuse the reader by choosing the wrong word for the context of a sentence. Look at this example:

The angry woman strolled up to the man.

It would be unusual for an angry person to 'stroll' as stroll implies a gentle, quite slow walk. If someone was angry we would expect their actions to be fast, furious and purposeful.

The angry woman marched up to the man.

In this example the emotion of the woman and the action of her movement match. The verb 'to march' implies a purposeful, direct action which is suitable for her emotion.

Take some time to choose your words – try not to just write down the first words that come to mind. By placing the right word in the right place, you will strengthen your writing and make your intentions clear to the reader.

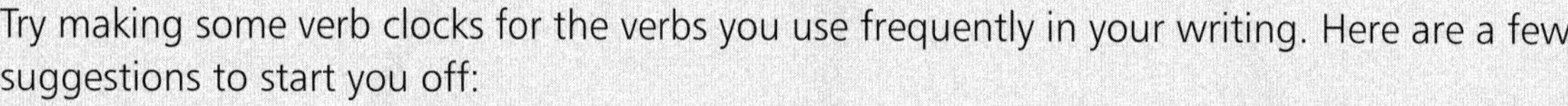

Now it's your turn!

Try making some verb clocks for the verbs you use frequently in your writing. Here are a few suggestions to start you off:

say

hit

take

like

want

Remember to check your thesaurus if you run out of ideas for alternative verbs.

2 As adverbs describe verbs they help to provide the reader with a clearer image and understanding of what is being described. As a result, it is important to have an extensive pool of adverbs to draw on in your writing.

An ideal method for expanding your knowledge of adverb groups is to build adverb ladders and your notebook is the perfect place to collate them.

- *First, choose an adverb and place it on the bottom rung of the ladder.*
- *Next, think of a similar adverb (a synonym) to write on the rung above.*

- *Then continue adding an adverb with a similar meaning to each rung and see how tall you can make the ladder.*
- *Finally, learn the adverb group so that you can draw on the full range when you need them for your writing.*

To show you how this technique works, here is an example of an adverb ladder built up from the word 'softly':

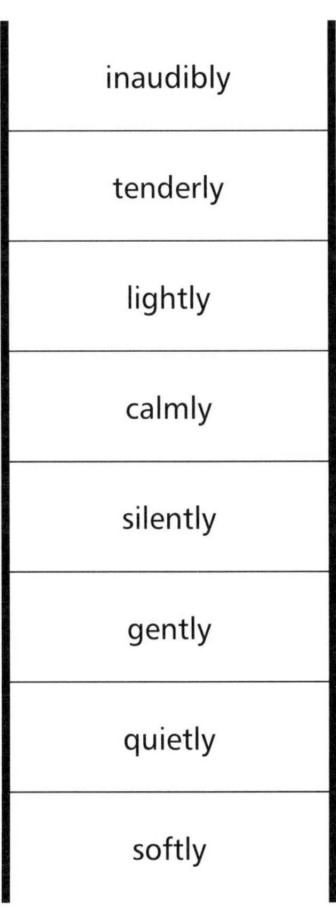

As with verbs, you need to choose your adverbs carefully to ensure that you create the image you want and that you avoid any confusion for the reader. For example:

The girl crept **quietly** *up the staircase.*

The image in this sentence is clear as 'quietly' is a sensible partner for the verb 'to creep'. Now watch what happens if a less appropriate adverb is used:

The girl crept **loudly** *up the staircase.*

This changes the image in the mind's eye and it no longer seems to make sense as the meaning of the verb 'to creep' is 'to move slowly and carefully, especially to avoid being noticed'. The adverb 'loudly' contradicts this idea so appears confusing for the reader.

When choosing which adverbs to include in your writing, also think about whether more than one word is needed in order to fully describe your scene. For example:

The girl crept **quietly** *and* **sneakily** *up the staircase.*

This suggests not only that the girl was trying hard not to make a noise but also that she was either going somewhere she shouldn't have been or perhaps that she was about to get into some mischief!

Top Tip

This game is a fun way of encouraging you to think about how words can be grouped together to create effects and it will also help you to develop a more varied vocabulary. You should first try to think of ideas yourself, but if you get stuck, you can turn to the dictionary for help.

1 First, write a name and a verb for each letter of the alphabet. For example: **Andrew abseils**.

2 Next, add an appropriate adjective to the noun: **Active Andrew abseils**.

3 Finally, add a relevant adverb to the verb: **Active Andrew abseils appallingly**.

For more of a challenge, why not race against someone and be the first to create a sensible sentence for each letter?

3 Adjectives are another key tool for a writer as, by describing nouns, they add vital details to mental pictures. It is therefore essential to build up your knowledge of adjectives so that you are able to inject these aspects of interest and detail into your own writing.

A successful way of collating groups of similar adjectives together is to form adjective grids. Again, your notebook is the best place to store these so that you can refer to them whenever you need to.

- *First, draw a 3x3 grid and place an adjective that you include regularly in your writing in the central box.*
- *Next, look up the adjective in a dictionary and thesaurus and choose a context that the word might be used in.*
- *Then, find up to eight synonyms that could replace the adjective in this context and note them down in the grid.*
- *Once you have completed one grid, you can then make similar grids containing synonyms that could replace the same adjective in the other contexts listed.*

So, for a common adjective such as 'good', this process might start as follows:

Good might be used in the context of:
- a good product
- a good condition
- a good person
- a good thing

- a good friend
- a good reason
- good behaviour
- a good time
- good food
- good weather

Top Tip

Remember that the context is the vital clue in finding the right adjective, so always check that your sentence makes sense.

Taking the context of 'a good product', good could be replaced with any of the following adjectives:

excellent	outstanding	wonderful
acceptable	**GOOD**	quality
fabulous	fantastic	superb

You might then start a new grid, listing synonyms that could replace good in the context of 'good weather' and so on.

Now it's your turn!

Find up to eight synonyms that could replace the adjective 'bad' in each of the following contexts, completing a separate grid for each group in your notebook.

- bad work
- bad food
- a bad time
- a bad back
- bad news
- bad luck
- a bad score
- bad manners

Now try to complete adjective grids for a range of other commonly used adjectives. Here are a few to start you off:

- little
- big
- old

Top Tip

Having a fantastic secret notebook that is packed with words, phrases and ideas is a waste unless you use it. Keep it with you so that you can note down and learn a new word (or phrase) every day. Then, to keep it fresh in your mind, try to use it in conversation and include it in your writing regularly.

d) *Think about the strength of meaning*

Top Tip

By adding just one new word a day you can increase your writing and speaking vocabulary by up to 31 words per month, which amounts to a massive 365 words in just one year!

Unfortunately, having a broad pool of verbs, adverbs and adjectives to draw on is not enough to guarantee a coherent and engaging piece of writing. You also need to consider the strength of the words you choose to ensure that they are appropriate for how and where you want to use them. Put simply, the more powerful the verb, adverb and adjective, the more powerful the statement and therefore the image it creates.

This is an important point to remember as you don't want to reduce the effect of your key sections of text by making everything sound too intense or extreme, but you also want to avoid boring your reader by not stating the main elements powerfully enough. To ensure that your writing offers an enjoyable and an engaging reading experience, you need to include a balance of both basic and powerful statements. This will help to create a 'rise and fall' or an 'ebb and flow' effect in your writing.

Look at the example extracts below:

> ## Extract A
>
> *The sky was the most fantastically deep blue with the whitest, fluffiest clouds he had ever seen. He woke feeling so amazing that morning, but now that he was outside, the extremely beautiful garden took his breath away. The superbly coloured flowers with such exotic scents swayed so beautifully in the perfectly gentle breeze that it was as much as he could do not to cry. The most gorgeous, sweet-faced little kitten that you could ever wish to meet was mewing with a resonant timbre that filled the garden like angels' harps.*

> ## Extract B
>
> *The sky was blue with white clouds. He was outside in the garden. The flowers swayed and a kitten mewed.*

When reading Extract A you should have noticed the extreme intensity with which every element and feeling is described. Too many powerful vocabulary terms have been used here, so no single incident or element really stands out from the next. If a whole letter, poem, magazine article or book was written at this level, the reader would soon become overwhelmed and stop reading.

By comparison, the text in Extract B is understated and minimal, providing only basic facts from which the reader would find it difficult to develop a full picture of the scene. It is likely that a complete letter, article, or book written in this format would therefore be quite short and bland and would prove difficult for the reader to engage with.

Let's have a look at a third version of the same description:

> ## Extract C
>
> *The sky was a deep blue with white, fluffy clouds. He woke that morning feeling happy, but now that he was outside, the beautiful garden took his breath away. The vivid flowers, with their exotic scents, swayed in the gentle breeze. A sweet-faced little kitten was mewing with a sound that filled the garden.*

You should have found Extract C much easier to read because it includes just enough detail to spark off the imagination. It avoids exaggerated extremes: 'A sweet-faced little kitten', not 'The most gorgeous, sweet-faced little kitten that you could ever wish to meet'; and the more descriptive sections: 'The sky was a deep blue with white, fluffy clouds …' and 'The vivid flowers, with their exotic scents, …' are also linked together with more basic statements: 'He woke that morning feeling happy …'.

This is an important technique to try and use in your writing, as it will not only help to create that rhythmic sense of 'ebb and flow' that will engage your reader but it will also allow you, as the writer, to place emphasis on specific sentences or sections of writing. This means that you can direct the reader's attention to particular sections of text.

One of the best ways to assess the intensity of descriptive words is to construct 'superlative staircases'. You can create these diagrams for any group of verbs, adverbs or adjectives and looking at where a particular word is placed on its staircase should really help you to think about the strength of its meaning before you use it in your writing.

Look at the example below:

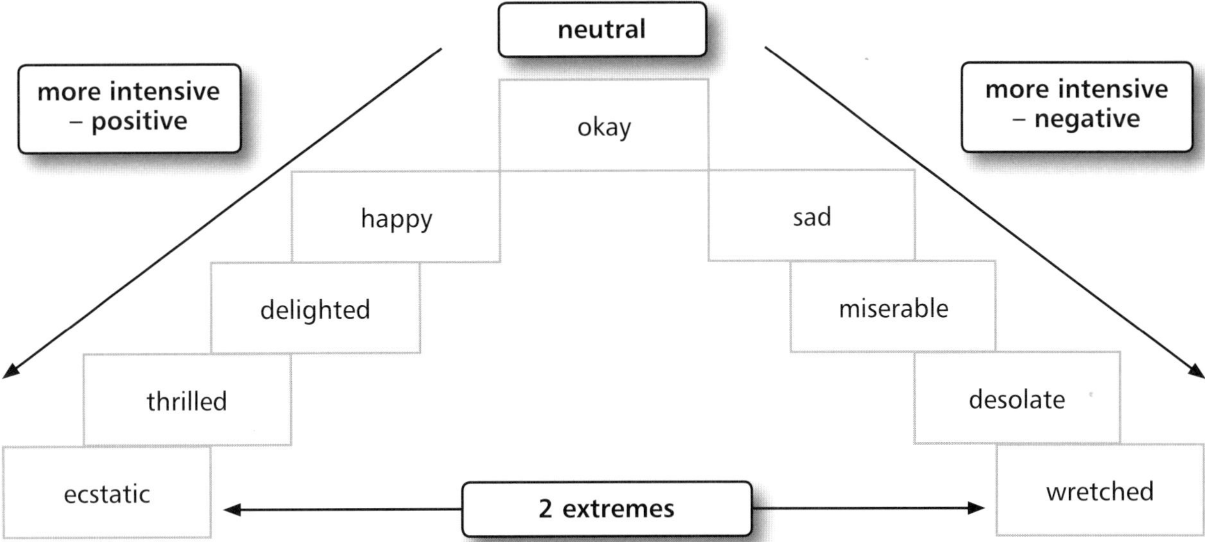

- *First, the neutral adjective 'okay' was placed on the central step.*
- *Next, four related adjectives were placed on the left-hand set of steps, positioned so that the level of intensity of positive feeling increases from top to bottom.*
- *Then, four more related adjectives were placed on the right-hand set of steps, but this time they show an increasing level of negative feeling from top to bottom.*

These nine steps clearly represent a spectrum of feelings, from one extreme, 'ecstatic', to another, 'wretched'. This isn't a task about finding exact opposites (antonyms), however. The aim of these 'staircases' is to encourage you to think about the strength of your chosen words so that you can gauge how and where best to include them in any piece of writing.

For example, you might want to use more powerful words as you move towards a climax or dramatic moment in a story. A woman might have felt *sad* when she found that her dog was missing, but she may have felt *wretched* after she searched for a week and found no trace of him. She might have been *delighted* to hear from someone who thought that they had seen the dog, but *ecstatic* when she finally found him.

Top Tip

Don't be afraid to draw on the full spectrum of words, but keep the extremes for points which really require exaggerated language or for occasions when you want to draw a reader's full attention to something.

Building up momentum in this way makes for powerful writing, but try to remember that your reader will find it tiring to read about extremes all of the time. Similarly, they may feel no connection to your writing at all if you never alter the intensity of the atmosphere or of your characters' feelings or actions.

e) *Introduce the senses*

As we explored in 'Planning a narrative' (pages 57–64), adding details of what can be seen, heard, tasted, smelled, physically touched or emotionally felt can really enhance a reader's experience of a piece of writing. Whether you use these elements to describe a character, an event or to place a fact within context, you should be able to bring a wide range of 'sense words' to mind quickly while you write.

One of the best ways to do this is to record as many words as you can in your notebook that relate to one of our five main senses: touch, taste, sight, smell and hearing. Words and phrases relating to a sixth sense, our sense of emotion, will also be useful in your writing. Note these words down in a way that will help you to recall them easily – below are some suggestions for methods you might like to try.

1 Group them in columns under the relevant sense headings, for example:

Touch	Taste	Sight	Smell	Hearing	Emotion
velvety	tangy	multi-coloured	odourless	hoot	happy
coarse	mouth-watering	transparent	perfumed	screech	anxious
cold	sweet	dull	fishy	crackle	terrified

2 Collate them in individual spider diagrams, for example:

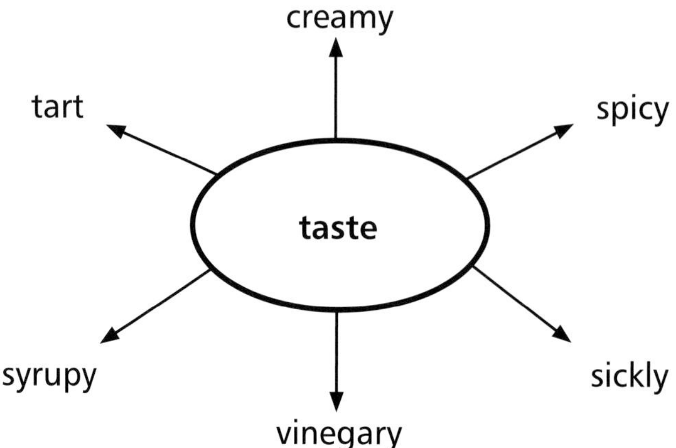

3 Create superlative staircases for a range of sense word extremes. Look back at 'Consider the strength of meaning' (pages 97–100) for more details about forming superlative staircases and a worked example.

 f Create the right image

This doesn't mean creating the right personal image – don't rush off and change your hairstyle or get some new clothes! As we have seen throughout the 'Develop language skills' section so far, the words that you use to describe something, as well as the level of detail you include, play a vital role in helping the reader to visualise (imagine) a scene.

The aim of this segment is to get you thinking about the different types of imagery (similes, metaphors and personification), common expressions and proverbs that you can use to help make your writing sparkle.

Similes

Similes are used to compare two things, either by using the term 'like' or the phrase 'as … as'. It is likely that you already know a number of similes so, starting with those you are familiar with, try to build up a broad collection. If you're not sure if you know any similes, here are some of the most common ones to start you off:

- **as** busy **as** a bee
- **as** cold **as** ice
- **as** cute **as** a button
- **as** good **as** gold
- **as** light **as** a feather
- **as** mad **as** a hatter
- eat **like** a pig
- eyes **like** a hawk
- ride **like** the wind
- know something **like** the back of your hand

When you are really familiar with a wide range of similes, try to drop them into your writing, but remember:

- *Make sure that each simile makes sense in the context you want to use it in.*
- *You only need one or two; if you use too many they could overpower what you are saying and make your writing sound 'clichéd'.*
- *Similes are often best used in descriptive writing and poetry.*

To make your writing even more original, try creating some new similes. How about 'as cold as the North Pole' instead of 'as cold as ice', for example?

Metaphors

Unlike a simile, a metaphor does not make a direct comparison between two things. Instead, this part of speech applies a word or phrase to something that it is not literally related to; it describes something as if it were something else.

Look at this sentence: *The balls of cotton wool* drifted along the horizon.

Cotton wool balls are not found in the sky so this phrase must be referring to something else. How would you describe cotton wool balls? Perhaps you might think of words like soft, white and round? Now what objects might you find in the sky that could be described using these same words? Clouds! So when reading the metaphor, 'the balls of cotton wool', we are meant to understand that the phrase is describing the appearance of the clouds.

Metaphors can be difficult to form so remember to look out for them as you read and note down any that appeal to you. Like similes, metaphors are often best suited to creative writing, descriptive passages and poetry.

You may find that the same metaphors appear in different types of reading material – here are some common ones to look out for:

- *apple of my eye*
- *a field of dreams*
- *raining cats and dogs*
- *a sea of trouble*
- *life is a journey*

You might like to try creating your own metaphors in your notebook, so here is a useful way to note down your ideas:

- Think of an object (the sun, for example) and note it down in the centre of a page.
- On the left-hand side of the object, note down a range of words or phrases that explain what it is like – describing it literally.
- On the right-hand side, note down words or phrases that compare the object to something else – describing it figuratively.

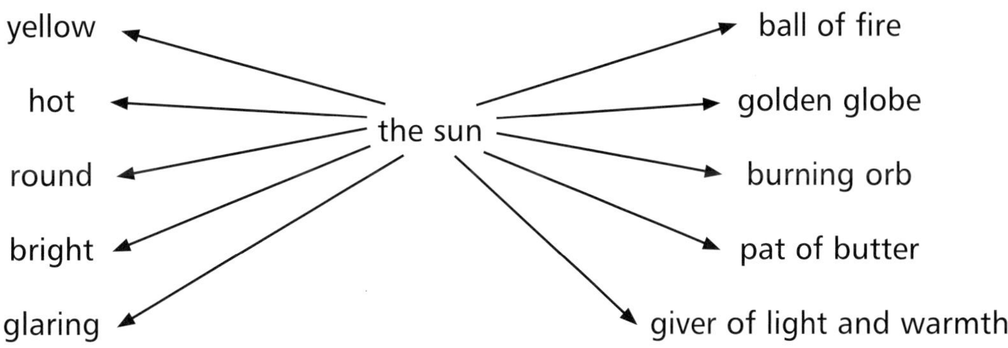

Splitting your descriptive words into literal and figurative groups like this, will help you to think about the different ways in which an object can be described as well as the different visual effect that a literal or figurative description will create in the reader's mind.

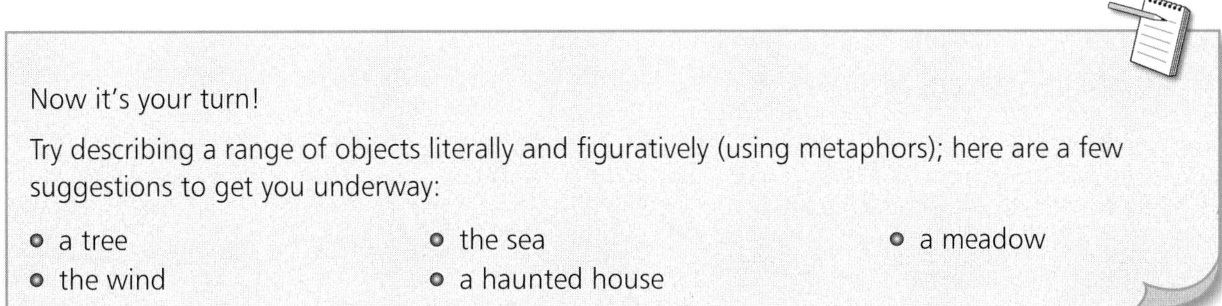

Now it's your turn!

Try describing a range of objects literally and figuratively (using metaphors); here are a few suggestions to get you underway:

- a tree
- the wind
- the sea
- a haunted house
- a meadow

Personification

Personification is a type of metaphor that gives human feelings, emotions or qualities to something that is non-human, such as an animal, a plant, a place or an object. Including this technique in a piece of writing can make a description stronger and create a more vivid image to help the reader connect with the element being described. It can often be tricky to spot elements of personification – it is common for writers to personify things without even realising it!

Let's look at some examples (the aspects of personification are in italics):

- The bluebells *bowed down respectfully* as we wandered along the path.
- The castle *sat proudly* at its post, *its steely eyes watching over* the vast lands below.
- The clouds *wept quietly* for most of the day.
- The engine *coughed* and *spluttered*.
- The floorboards *groaned* under the weight of the cupboard.
- The lighthouse *blinked slowly* in the fog.

Can you see how the subject of each sentence has been personified? The effect is that each image is implied rather than stated directly, meaning that the reader has to imagine the scenes being described. In the third sentence, for example, the clouds are described as 'weeping', but people cry, not clouds. The use of personification here implies that it rained for most of the day.

Personification is often found in descriptive writing. It can be an effective technique but is one that should be used sparingly to ensure that the reader's attention is drawn to key aspects of the text when required. If everything is described in this way, then the dramatic effect will be lost. You should also take a little time to think about whether the human characteristics or emotions that you want to apply to the non-human object are actually appropriate.

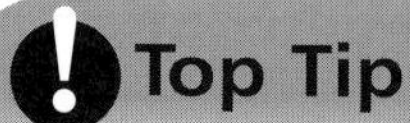

Top Tip

Look out for verbs that imply human actions or emotions as you read. If they have been used to describe something non-human, then they are examples of personification.

Rewrite each of these sentences using personification to describe the given scenarios. An example has been given to start you off.

The bumble bee flew from one flower to the next.
The bumble bee skipped along from one flower to the next.

1 The cat jumped on to the fence.

____

2 The tractor rattled across the field.

____

3 The wind caused the umbrella to turn inside out.

____

4 The fruit bowl was in the middle of the table.

____

Expressions and sayings

There are many common expressions and sayings that are often used to enrich our language. Many come from the Bible, while others originate from advertising slogans, newspapers or television programmes. Some are taken from the works of literary writers such as Shakespeare, others can be traced back to historical or maritime origins.

Top Tip

Expressions and sayings are very useful for adding a sense of realism in playscripts or in other forms of dialogue.

Let's look at some examples and their meanings. You may be more familiar with some expressions than you realise!

Expression	Meaning	Expression	Meaning
break a leg	good luck	once in a blue moon	rarely
blow your own trumpet	be boastful	all fingers and thumbs	being clumsy
away with the fairies	daydreaming	sitting on the fence	can't make a decision

We often say or write such common sayings without realising, so keep your eyes and ears open for different sayings as you hear people talk or read different materials.

Now it's your turn!

Find one expression from the list below to complete each sentence correctly.

- cut off your nose to spite your face
- your eyes are bigger than your stomach
- Bob's your uncle
- just play it by ear
- cheap at half the price
- more fool you
- sent to Coventry
- back to basics
- vanished into thin air
- over the moon
- making a right pig's ear of it
- flying by the seat of your pants

1 All you have to do is plug the lead into the socket and _______________________.

2 I bought it for five pounds which is _______________________.

3 You're full because _______________________.

4 By the time I'd turned the corner he'd _______________________.

5 I was _______________________ when I won the competition.

Proverbs

A proverb is another type of common saying that is used regularly by writers and speakers to enrich their language and to create a particular image in the mind of the reader or listener.

Like other expressions, we often say them without realising – possibly because they have been passed down from one generation to the next and we are so familiar with them. They can help to create realism in all forms of dialogue and can also be ideal for occasions when you want to use just a few words to explain a more detailed idea.

Here are some examples of common proverbs.

- *A fool and his money are soon parted.*
- *Bad new travels fast.*
- *Don't look a gift horse in the mouth.*
- *A penny saved is a penny earned.*
- *The best things in life are free.*
- *The grass is always greener on the other side.*
- *Don't keep a dog and bark yourself.*

Look or listen out for interesting examples of proverbs when people are talking or while you are reading. Note down as many as you can in your notebook so that you can build up a broad collection to use in your own writing.

However, do check that you know what each proverb means before using it – a proverb that is inappropriate for the context will confuse your reader. Remember also that you only need to include one or two proverbs in a piece of writing. If you try to add too many, your text will become hard to follow and your reader will quickly become tired!

Now it's your turn!

Can you match each proverb with its definition?

1 Birds of a feather flock together.
2 Nothing ventured, nothing gained.
3 Where there's a will, there's a way.
4 Every cloud has a silver lining.
5 A stitch in time saves nine.
6 Out of the frying pan, into the fire.

a *Something good will come out of even a very bad situation.*
b *If you really want to do something, you'll work out how to do it.*
c *It is better to do a job now, as it will only get worse later.*
d *People congregate with others who have similar interests.*
e *You solve one bad situation and end up in one that is even worse.*
f *You can't be rewarded for something if you don't try.*

Consider presentation

a *Check your answer*

All writers should check through their work before submitting it to someone to be read or marked. Even professional authors and writers have their texts proofread for errors, sense and accuracy before they are published. Unfortunately, in an exam, you cannot ask anyone else to check your work, so you need to make sure that you know what to look out for and that you leave enough time to check back through your writing. Try to remember to check through every practice writing task you do – then it will be an automatic process for you in an exam.

The following points will act as helpful reminders for you. No matter what type of task you have chosen, check that your writing:

- *relates to the title prompt throughout – have you lost focus part way through?*
- *is structured appropriately – remember, for example, that even a simple story needs a beginning, middle and end*
- *is organised properly – have you written in sentences, used clear paragraphs or gathered ideas under appropriate headings?*
- *is interesting or entertaining for the reader – a good tip is that if you had fun writing your answer, then your reader should enjoy it too!*
- *states what you want it to, accurately – check that your spellings and use of grammar and punctuation are correct*
- *is legible – have you used your best handwriting so that the reader can clearly see what you have written?*
- *avoids repetition – if, for example, every sentence starts with 'I' your writing will quickly become quite dull to read. Try to make sure that you use a wide selection of sentence openings (such as time connectives) as well as synonyms and antonyms to create a sense of variety and interest throughout your work.*
- *is written in Standard English – unless a prompt implies that the use of slang or colloquial language would be appropriate, try to avoid using these styles of text in your writing.*

Never be scared to make changes. Teachers and examiners like to see that you have checked and proofread your work but make sure that any changes you make are neat and legible. For example, if you need to change a word, cross out the original word with a simple horizontal line and write the new word above it.

If you need to change more than one or two words, or want to add more information to your text, then place an asterisk (*) at the point where you want to include the new text and write the missing content at the top or bottom of the page (wherever there is more room). If, however, you find that there are several places where you want to add more material, use numbers rather than an asterisk to indicate where each new piece of text fits in to your original writing. For clarity, it may be useful to circle each number so it stands out in the text.

Using any of these correction techniques will ensure that your work remains as neat and easy to read as possible. They will also help you to keep track of any changes that you make to your work.

! Top Tip

When checking through any practice writing task, you might find it helpful to read your work aloud. Reading and listening to what you have written can often allow you to quickly identify any problems with spelling, sentence structures or use of punctuation, for example. It will also help you to make sure that what you have written makes sense.

b Examine your handwriting

Like reading and spelling, handwriting is a key skill that boosts written communication across all subject areas. By the end of Year 6, it is important for all children to have developed their own legible, fluent and joined style of handwriting. This is not just to make it easier and quicker to complete tests or exams, but it will also be valuable preparation for all written tasks in secondary school and beyond.

Handwriting can be described as a 'movement' skill because it involves using a series of flowing movements and patterns to make marks on the page. It is a process that can be difficult to master at first but don't worry; it should eventually become automatic for you – allowing you to think freely about what you are writing instead of focusing on how you are writing it. However, it takes a lot of practice to get to this point so try to practise your handwriting as much as possible both in school and at home.

Top Tip

Practising little and often is best – writing in short sessions will help to stop you and your hand getting too tired!

✓ **Parent Tip**

Your child's school should have a handwriting policy – ask for information on this and for ways in which you can help to support their handwriting development.

Below are some useful hints and ideas that will help you to practise and improve your handwriting.

1 When you are writing, think about your:

- **grip** – *how are you holding the pen or pencil? It should be between your thumb and first finger and resting against your middle finger*
- **posture** – *are you sitting comfortably or is your neck or back aching? Ask someone to check that your shoulders are not slumping forward and that the height of the table and chair are correct for you*
- **paper** – *is it in the right position for you? If you are right-handed then your paper should be placed to your right; if you are left-handed then it should be to your left. It is also often helpful to place your paper at a slight angle (rather than it lying straight) and to use your non-writing hand to stop the paper from moving around as you write*
- **writing space** – *is there enough room around you to write comfortably? Make sure that you have plenty of 'elbow room' and space to spread out when you are writing.*

2 Try some or all of these tasks:

Experiment with a wide variety of writing implements (such as pencils, ballpoint pens, felt tip pens, calligraphy pens and fountain pens) – how does your writing style change with each one?	Test your memory – try writing your name, address and some simple sentences with your eyes closed. This is an excellent way to focus on how each letter is formed.	Swap a piece of your handwriting with someone else's – have you both formed your letters correctly? Have you both been consistent in the size, proportion and spacing of your letters?	Borrow some calligraphy books from the library – these will have some wonderful ideas for practising different writing styles and creating lovely patterns and borders around your work.

Use joined up handwriting for all of your writing, unless it is not appropriate to do so. This style of writing looks more grown up and it is also faster to write in this way as you do not need to lift the nib off the paper.

Stock up on handwriting paper – this will help to remind you about the size and position of your ascenders (heads), descenders (tails), loops and slants.

Draw or paint different patterns – these techniques will help you to practise free-flowing hand movements.

Look at the different fonts and writing styles in a word processing package – this should help to remind you that the presentation of any piece of work is important.

Have fun with writing games and puzzles (such as Hangman and crosswords).

Time yourself when copying out poems or narrative passages in your best handwriting.

Follow the handwriting exercises in the *Bond No Nonsense English* books designed for 5–11 year-olds.

Make a writing box – fill it with lots of coloured paper; different types of pens and pencils; a sheet of writing guidelines (this can be placed underneath a piece of plain paper so that the dark lines will show through the top sheet and you can use them as a guide to create neat, straight lines of writing); craft materials that you can use to frame some examples of your best handwriting or turn them into a book.

 Top Tip

You may have written a wonderful piece of writing that is worth full marks, but if no one can read it then all of your efforts will be wasted! Remember to write quickly but clearly at all times.

✓ Parent Tip

HB pencils are recommended if children want to practise writing with a pencil, and triangular 'grip' pencils are easier to hold.

3 If you write with your left hand then you might sometimes find yourself struggling with:

- **position** – *often left-handed writers 'hook' their hand around the pen or pencil so that their hand is above the implement and their line of writing. This can put their arm and body into an awkward position that makes it feel uncomfortable and slow to write*
- **grip** – *it is common for left-handed people to hold their pen or pencil very tightly. This usually results in poor handwriting (letters might be formed badly for example) and can make it very tiring to write*
- **smudged work** – *this can often be the result of the 'hooked' hand position, as the writing hand follows on behind the writing implement and passes over what has just been written*
- **mirror-writing** – *the standard way of reading and writing is to work across a page from left to right. However, many left-handed writers will instinctively start at the right-hand margin and work across to the left-hand side of the page. Usually this will also mean that they will write words back to front.*

Don't worry if you find yourself grappling with any of these aspects from time to time; they are common problems for all left-handed people. Some of the following ideas might help:

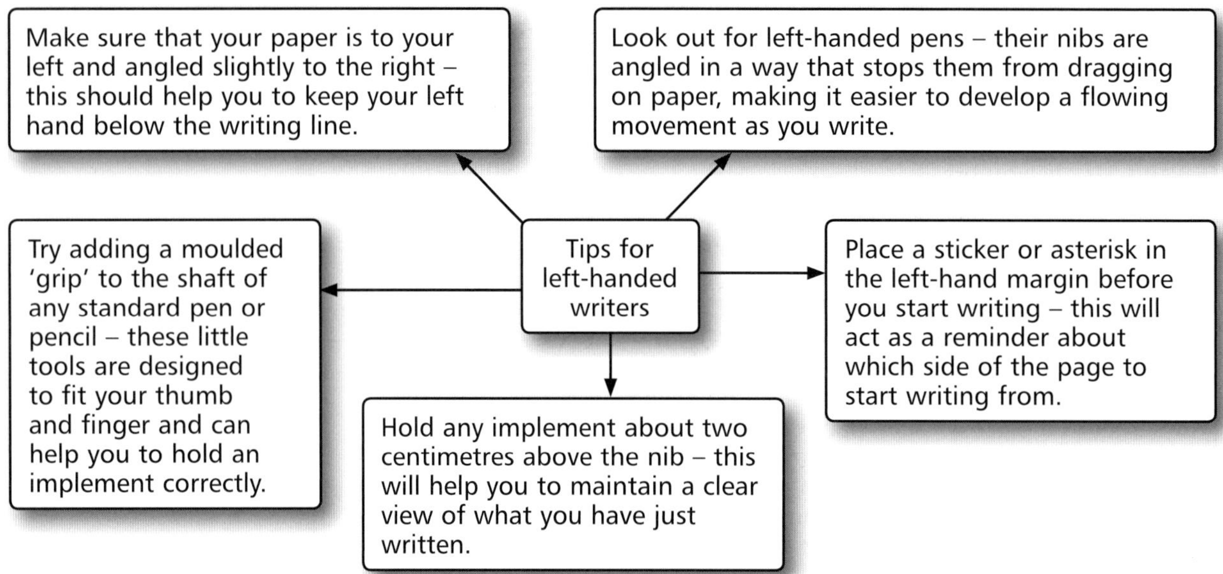

Now it's your turn!

Practise writing every letter of the alphabet by copying out each sentence below in your best handwriting. When you have written them all ask someone to look at your handwriting and comment on your letter formation as well as consistency of size and spacing. Then try to write them again, remembering the feedback you have been given.

Compare your first and second attempts. If you need further practice, try the exercise again. If you are happy with your handwriting then set yourself a challenge – write them out again but, on this attempt, time yourself to see how fast you can copy the sentences in neat and legible handwriting. Don't be tempted to swap tidiness for speed!

1 Schoolboy providing serious answer to joke question, wins the maximum five prizes.
2 Six big, cheeky monkeys have jumped out. Keep quiet while I fetch the zookeeper.
3 To map reader's joy, hazy sunshine broke waxen clouds of quilted fog.
4 Came joint seventh with extra prize for equally special handwriting book.
5 Extremely quick badger had a very fuzzy coat and sharp, jointed claws.
6 Joy's hot fire blazed quickly, while cooking smells proved extremely irresistible.

✓ **Parent Tip**

Printable worksheets with letter guides that offer further handwriting practice can be downloaded from: www.handwritingworksheets.com

● Assess your speed

The time allowed for an examined writing task may be anywhere between 30 minutes and 1 hour 15 minutes. It can be hard to get a sense of what large blocks of time like these actually 'feel' like, so a helpful technique to try is breaking practice sessions down into shorter time blocks. You could do this either by setting an alarm clock or by asking someone else to watch the time and to tell you when to move on to the next stage of writing preparation.

To give you a sense of how this timing method could work, below are some suggested time frames for each writing stage (based on a time limit of 40 minutes). You can adapt this suggested structure for any time limit.

Read any given instructions carefully before you start, then keep an eye on the time as you write. Try not to spend so much time clock-watching that you run out of time to finish your writing though!

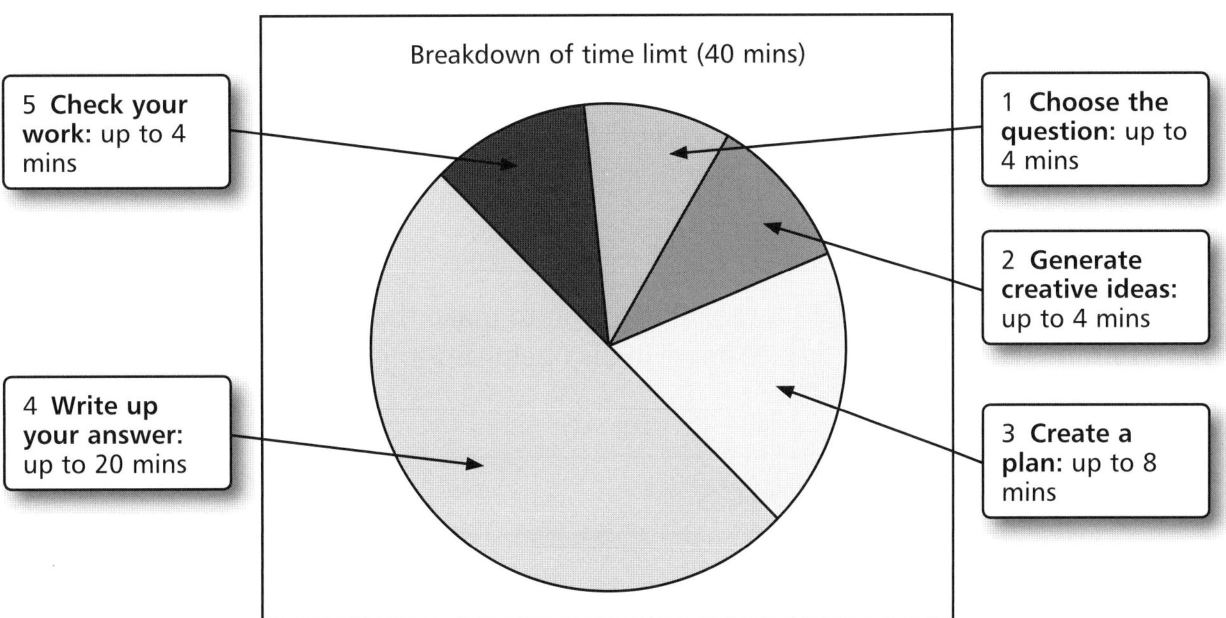

Don't panic if, when you look at this pie chart, you feel there is very little time to complete each stage. It is difficult for most children and adults to get their timings right for the first few attempts at any timed task. The best thing you can do is practice, practice, practice. Here is a useful checklist that you can refer to before each timed practice session that you do:

- *First, make sure that you have a quiet, well-lit place to sit. If you need to have a drink or use the toilet, now is the time before your timed session begins.*
- *Then, check that everyone knows you are going to work through a timed task so that you are not interrupted part way through – now is the time to turn off mobile phones!*
- *Next, place a watch or an alarm clock nearby so that you can keep an eye on the time. As mentioned above, an alarm clock is ideal as you can set it to ring when it is time to move on to each writing stage. However, you may prefer to ask someone to give you some verbal time checks at these points so that you don't have to keep breaking off from your task to reset the alarm.*

Don't worry if the time runs out before you have finished your task. This might happen several times before you start to get familiar with how short blocks of time 'feel'. If this happens to you, just put a mark in the margin next to the point you had reached when the time ran out and then continue with your writing. Completing the task will help you to see how far you were from the end and how much more time you would have needed to finish.

Once you have finished writing, think back through the task and try to work out where you spent most of your time. Asking yourself questions such as those below could be helpful in working out which sections took you the longest to write.

- *How long did I take to choose my task? Do I need more practice at recognising a title prompt?*
- *How long did I spend planning? Do I need more practice at techniques that will help me to generate ideas quickly?*
- *How much did I write? Were all of the details I included actually necessary to complete the task? Did I stick to the task or lose focus part way through?*
- *How long did I spend checking my work? Did I rush through my writing and then have to make a lot of changes?*

Top Tip

Remember, it's quality, not quantity that will ultimately achieve the highest marks.

Thinking about questions like these will help you to make the best use of the time you have for any type of writing task. They will also help you to gradually pace yourself as you prepare your answers.

3 | Boost the basics

● Succeed in spelling

Many people (adults as well as children) find spelling English words difficult because the way that words are spelt is often different from how they are pronounced. This is largely because, over many years, English has been influenced by different languages (such as French, Latin and German). With the increased use of 'quick forms of communication' such as text messaging and emails, the use of standard spellings has also declined.

Spelling is an important skill for everyone to have as it helps to boost reading, writing and communication skills as well as expanding vocabulary knowledge. You will already know how to spell many words through talking, reading lots of books, watching television and learning a regular list of spellings from school. However, don't worry if you find some words more difficult to remember and spell than others. No one is expecting you to spell every word that you write correctly but you should feel confident with most of the words that you use in your writing at this stage.

Having a broad spelling knowledge not only increases your chance of getting a good mark for any piece of written work, but it will also make you more confident at writing in general.

To help you meet some of the key goals that children are expected to achieve by the time they leave primary school, here are some brief reminders of some common rules that are good to know as well as some ideas and tips to help make spellings stick (and make them fun!).

(a) *Apply common spelling rules*

One of the reasons that many people struggle with learning English is that there are lots of rules to learn about how certain words are formed. Unfortunately, for every rule, there are also likely to be several words that do not follow them, so this makes it even harder to remember particular spellings! However, do your best to learn the rules as they will help you with many words.

Five of the main sets of rules that you should know are briefly outlined in the diagram below.

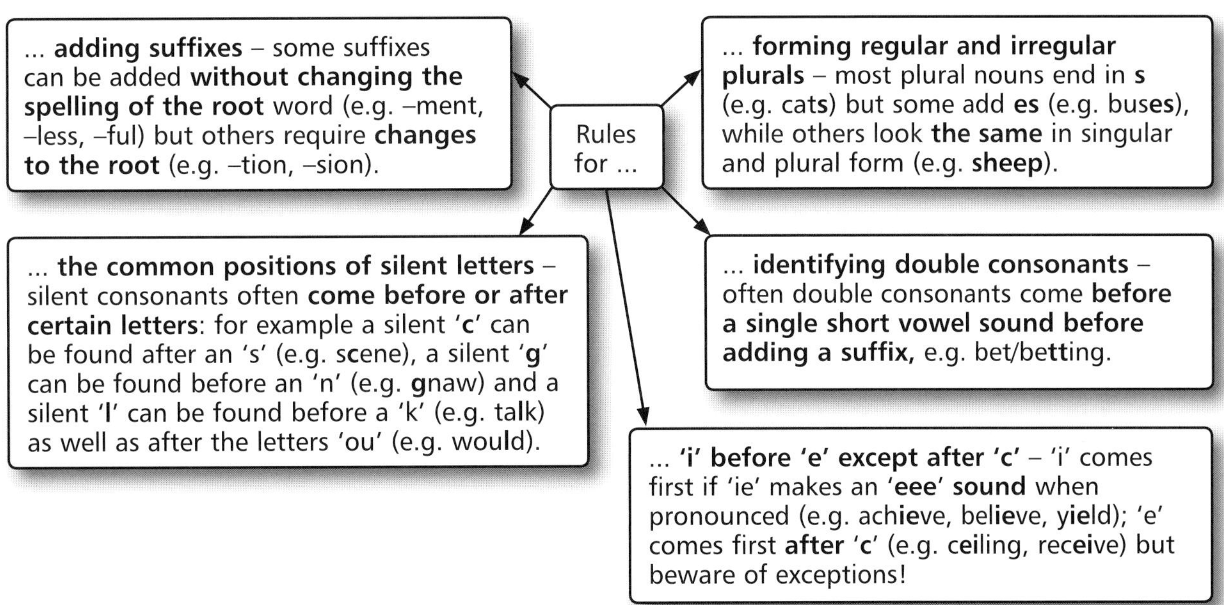

If you need a more detailed reminder of some or all of these common spelling rules, then work through the spelling section in *Bond How to do ... 11⁺ English* (see the Additional resources appendix in section C for details). This has a lot of helpful explanations and practice activities for all of these rules and much more.

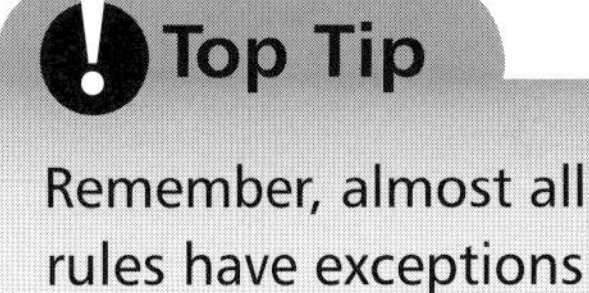

(b) *Spell familiar words correctly/Use a range of strategies to spell difficult and unfamiliar words*

These two goals have been grouped together in this section as the wide range of techniques and tips given below will be ideal for reinforcing familiar words as well as for learning how to spell more difficult or unfamiliar ones. Have a go at each suggestion. You may find that you prefer some ideas and techniques to others – that's fine, practise the spelling methods that work for you!

You might find it useful to copy these ideas out on to sticky notes and put them around your bedroom so that you can remind yourself to try a different one each day.

Look, Say, Cover, Write, Check (LSCWC)

Looking at words is an important part of learning to spell them. Take time to look at the shape of a word and the individual letters it is made up from. Always ask yourself if a word 'looks right'. The LSCWC method is ideal for practising the 'looking' technique and for writing the shape of the word from memory.

1 Look closely at the word.
2 Say the word out loud or in your head.
3 Cover the word up (if it is on a spelling list you can turn the paper over).
4 Write the word from memory.
5 Check your spelling against the original word.

Increase your vocabulary

Aim to learn 10 new words per week on top of your weekly school spelling list. You might pick these out of a dictionary or thesaurus or from a spelling list such as *Schonell's Essential Spelling List* (see Additional resources appendix). Copy them into your notebook and then ask someone to test you regularly – write out any that you get wrong at least five times to help you to recall the correct spellings.

Be creative

Choose five of your favourite words or five of those that you find difficult to spell and use them in a short piece of writing. Then highlight them in some way (perhaps write them, circle them or underline them in a different colour) so that they stand out from the text.

Identify smaller components

If you get stuck on an unfamiliar word, try looking for smaller words within it (e.g. opportunity contains 'port' and 'unity'). To get used to looking for words within words, choose any word ('father' for example) and find as many smaller words as possible within it (fat / at / the / he / her). For more of a challenge, try doing this against the clock, or race someone to find the most words.

Use syllables and sound

Split a word into syllables, which you can separate using a forward slash mark, and then sound out each section. Write the number of syllables that each word contains in brackets after the word (e.g. Wed / nes / day (3)). This will help you to see the shape of the word and the letters that it is made up from more clearly. Remember though, that some words will be pronounced differently when all of the syllables are put together.

Create mnemonics

Making up mnemonics (short rhymes, phrases or poems) can often make many different types of information easier to memorise and recall. These types of memory aids work particularly well for awkward spellings. Here are some examples for you to try out but have a go at making up your own for words that you find hard to spell:

Big **E**mus **A**re **U**nusually **beau**tiful.
Every **busi**ness has its own **bus**.
Rob, **R**on, **S**ally and **S**ean were asked to spell emba**rrass**.
Una and **A**li's birthdays are in the middle of Febr**ua**ry.
Friday comes at the **end** of every school week (friend).
One camel and **two s**nakes are ne**cess**ary, or **N**aughty **E**lla **C**an **E**at **S**even **S**ausages **A**nd **R**unny **Y**oghurt.
There is **a rat** in sep**arat**e.
Two 'c's and **two** 's's will lead to su**cce**ss.

Little gems

Try writing words out in fancy writing (perhaps using a calligraphy pen) and then make them into a poster to look at each day.

For unfamiliar words, look for an element that you recognise. This might be a common letter string, a root word, prefix or suffix, for example.

Dip into a dictionary and thesaurus regularly.

Make your own dictionary of difficult words.

Play word games, e.g. Boggle, Scrabble, Hangman, anagrams, wordsearches, and crosswords.

Draw a picture to represent part or all of a difficult word.

Read, read, read! The more you read, the more words you will recognise – reinforcing those that you already know and enabling you to make a note of any new or difficult words in your notebook as you come across them. Reading as widely as possible will also help you to check your own writing to make sure that each word 'looks right'.

Cut out interesting, unfamiliar or difficult words from magazines and stick them into your notebook. Or, cut out the letters from newspaper headlines and make new words with them.

 **Top Tip**

Write out any word that you misspell five times, using a different coloured pen or pencil each time.

 **Top Tip**

While you're getting ready for school can be a good time to attempt some spellings out loud!

c) *Group words according to spelling patterns*

Remember that all English words are formed using a mix of only 26 letters, so many words repeat the same letter combinations. It can make it easier to recall individual words if you group together and learn:

- *sets of similarly spelt words, either in diagrams or under column headings in a grid – remember that words which include the same letter string often have different pronunciations (e.g. **cough, rough, bough, ought**/**ear, heart, earth, bear**).*
- *words that include the same common letter string but which also sound the same – a grid or diagram would be ideal here too! (e.g. **claim, faint, hail, main, staid, wait**).*
- *words according to how they sound – remember that the same sound can be represented by many different spelling forms (e.g. **claw, floor, four, maul, store, sure, tall, war, water**). Again, you might choose to record these words in a table or in a spider diagram.*
- *words that contain the same silent or 'swallowed' vowels or consonants (e.g. silent **h**: anchor, ghost, rhyme, whistle) – these letters can be easy to forget and often catch people out. Another way to group them is to list them in their word families because other words in the same group may pronounce these letters and act as a useful reminder (e.g. silent **g** in sign v. signal, signature/'swallowed' first **'i'** in medicine v. medic, medical, medication).*

Look out for words that share the same letter strings as you read and highlight them with coloured pens or pencils. Use a different colour for each letter string. You can do the same when spotting silent or 'swallowed' letters.

(d) Recognise the spelling and meaning of common homophones

A homophone is a word that sounds the same as another word (or words) but it is spelt differently and its meaning is also different. These can cause a lot of confusion, particularly when words are being dictated, as you need to be able to understand the context of a sentence in order to work out which is the correct spelling to use.

Here are some pairs and groups of common homophones that often catch people out:

board/bored	its/it's	rain /reign/rein
caught/court	knew/new	stationary/stationery
for/four	passed/past	their/there/they're
grate/great	practice/practise	to/too/two
hole/whole	principal/principle	your/you're

There are lots of homophones so you need to try and learn as many as possible – both their spellings and their meanings. These ideas might help to make learning them more fun:

- *Someone says and spells one half of a homophone pair (or one from a group) and you then have to think of its homophone partner (or the rest of the group). You must spell the word(s) and also give the different meaning(s). Make a list of the words as you go so that you know which homophones you have used.*
- *Ask someone to write out pairs or groups of homophones on separate cards (or you could do this) and then turn them all over and mix them up. Take it in turns to pick two cards and try to match the homophone pairs. If you don't pick a pair, put the cards back. When you have a pair (or group) you must pronounce the words and explain their different meanings in order to keep them. The winner is the one with the most homophone pairs.*
- *As you read, look out for words that are homophones. Challenge someone (or yourself) to see how many you can circle in a newspaper or magazine article. Write out each word with its homophone partner(s) in the margin of the article or in your notebook.*
- *Mnemonics can also be useful for remembering the differences between the spellings and meanings of some homophones (e.g. An **envelope** is an item of station**e**ry/The **automobile** was station**a**ry.)*

Read through the spelling section in *Bond How to do … 11⁺ English* (pages 75–91). This also offers lots of advice on techniques to improve your spelling, as well as looking at some of the most common awkward word groups such as: homophones and homonyms, singulars and plurals, silent letters, prefixes and suffixes, common letter strings and double consonants. It also has lots of practice activities to try.

Grow your grammar

What do we mean by grammar? The term 'grammar' refers to the ways in which language is put together; how words and sentences are structured to create meaning. Like spelling, grammar is another area of English that many people continually struggle with because there are so many rules and different elements to try and learn. However, it is important to have a sound understanding of the main aspects of English grammar if you are going to write confidently and achieve high marks in any piece of writing that you produce.

If you get confused by grammar then don't worry; you probably know a lot more than you realise already through talking, listening, reading, writing and school literacy lessons. Work through this section to check how much you know about some of the core aspects that you need to be aware of by the time you leave primary school (e.g. phrases, clauses, sentences, parts of speech, subjects and objects).

If, when you have completed the section, you find that you need a more detailed reminder and more practice of any elements, read the grammar section in *Bond How to do … 11⁺ English* (page 48 onwards) and then work through the *Bond No Nonsense English* books (for 5–11 year-olds) and the range of *Bond English Assessment Papers* (for ages 5–13 years).

What do you know about …?

Sentences, phrases and clauses

1   A phrase must contain a subject and a verb. True or False? _________________

2   What must a sentence always start with? _________________

3   How many types of clause are there? Name the types. _________________

4   Sentences are made up of phrases and clauses. True or False? _________________

5   A sentence must always finish with a full stop. True or False? _________________

6   What type of clause starts with a connective? _________________

7   What must any sentence always contain? _________________

8   'a short journey home'. Is this an example of a phrase, clause or sentence? _________

9   Sentences can be short or long. True or False? _________________

10   How would you define the term 'complex sentence'? _________________

11   What type of clause makes sense on its own? _________________

12   What term is used to describe a sentence that describes someone or something doing something, rather than something being done to them? _________________

Parts of speech

1   Where would you expect to find a preposition in a sentence? Tick ONE option.
a after a noun   ☐   b after an adjective ☐   c before a verb   ☐
d before a noun ☐   e after a verb   ☐   f in between a noun and a verb ☐

2   List all of the different types of nouns and give an example of each one. ___________
____

3   The colour 'purple' is an adjective. True or False? _________________________________

4   Describe the term 'verb'. ____

5   What can a pronoun replace in a sentence? ______________________________________

6   What FOUR things can adverbs tell you about something? ___________________________

7   Give an example of a preposition that shows:
a position ____________   b time __________   c direction _____________

8   How are connectives used in sentences? ____

9   Give an example of an auxiliary verb in its infinitive form. _______________________

10 Which THREE terms are used to describe adjectives that compare things?
    Give an example of each type of comparing adjective. _____________________________
____

11 Which type of noun must always start with a capital letter? _______________________

12 What does the tense of a verb show? ____

13 How many types of pronoun are there? Give an example of each type. ________________
____

14 An adjective describes a verb. True or False? ____________________________________

15 Connectives can be one word or a short phrase. True or False? ____________________

Subjects and objects

1   Explain what the subject of a sentence is. ______________________________________

2   Define the object of a sentence. ____

3   What must the subject of a sentence agree with? _________________________________

4   The object of a sentence is always singular. True or False? _______________________

5   Which parts of speech would you normally expect to see as the subject of a
    sentence? ____

6   Underline the objects in these sentences:

a The Championship was won by the best football team.
b Chloë and I went down to the beach for a swim.
c Sandy knelt down and picked up her puzzle book.

7   Underline the subject in this sentence: Young Alice was always getting herself into trouble.

How did you find these questions? Ask someone to read through your answers with you before checking against the answers in the appendix. Make a note of any aspects that you were not sure about or couldn't answer and then look back at the 'Develop language skills' section (pages 86–106) for ideas about how to strengthen your knowledge about some of these elements. Also read through the detailed grammar section in Bond's *How to do … 11⁺ English*, which covers all of the core grammar points raised here.

Remember, the more confident you are in all aspects of grammar, the easier you will find it to answer any type of writing prompt.

● Practise your punctuation

Punctuation is used to separate sentences and words so that writing is clear and easy to read. If a section of text had no punctuation then the meaning of individual phrases and sentences would be lost and the whole piece would be very hard to understand. For example, a reader would find it difficult to detect any sense of rhythm, intonation, emotion, suspense, emphasis, speech or change in subject or theme – all things that can help to make text sparkle and which contribute to the reading experience. Each of these elements is supported by a specific punctuation mark and if these marks were omitted the content would appear dull, lifeless and confusing for the reader.

As with spelling and grammar, there are rules that punctuation marks follow. Each one has at least one specific job to do, so you can't just put different punctuation marks anywhere in a piece of text. In order to use them properly, and with confidence, you need to understand the main role (or roles) of every mark. You have probably found that it is easier to remember what some punctuation marks do compared to others, and if so, then don't worry. Punctuation is another tricky part of English that a lot of people struggle with.

Let's see how much you already know and which punctuation marks you might need to remind yourself about. A wide range of punctuation marks are shown below. Can you match the right punctuation mark to each of the job descriptions that follow? Write the appropriate term or symbol on the answer rule after each job role.

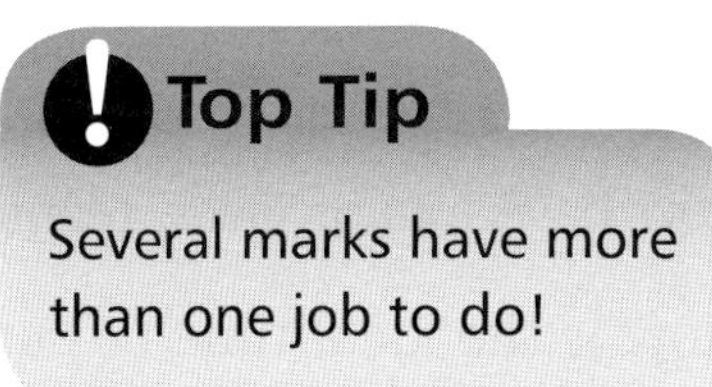

paragraph   !   …   ?   .   —   :   '   "   ,   -   ;   "   ( )

1   I can replace 'and' as well as 'or' to separate items in a simple list. ______
2   I join two or more complete sentences together in the place of a conjunction. ______
3   I can join some compound words together as well as some prefixes to root words. ______
4   I'm found after an exclamation. ______
5   I precede a list. ______
6   I work in a pair to separate abbreviations and numbers from the rest of a sentence. ______
7   I always follow a piece of dialogue. ______
8   I indicate a change in subject or theme in a piece of text. ______
9   I signify the end of a complete statement. ______

10 I indicate that a word has not fit fully onto a line._____

11 I always work in a pair and am often used to separate non-essential information from the rest of a sentence._____

12 I can separate a name or term of address from the rest of a sentence._____

13 I am placed after a question._____

14 I introduce an explanation of what has been said previously._____

15 I show possession._____

16 I show that a sentence has been left unfinished._____

17 I show where one or more letters are missing from a word._____

18 I am always placed before direct speech._____

19 I come at the end of an order._____

20 I can replace a different mark and am used to separate items in complex lists._____

21 I can work in a pair and am used regularly to separate clauses within a sentence._____

22 I separate statements of direct speech from pieces of narrative text._____

23 I show when someone different is talking in a piece of dialogue._____

24 I work in a pair and am used occasionally to separate non-essential information from the rest of a sentence._____

How did you do? For any punctuation marks that you feel you need more practice on, try the exercises in the *Bond No Nonsense English* series as well as in the range of *Bond Assessment Papers in English*. To brush up on the rules of when any of these marks are used, see the punctuation section in *Bond How to do ... 11⁺ English*.

Finally, remember to think carefully about what you are writing as you write. Make sure that you know what you want to say and then think about the punctuation marks that will help you to communicate the right meanings and effects to your reader. You may not always get it right – using punctuation can be quite a challenge, particularly in complex sentences – but the more you practise, the easier it will become.

Final thoughts

I hope that you have found this book an informative and useful resource and that you will now have lots of ideas, techniques and strategies for performing well in writing tasks.

Now is the ideal time to put what you have learned into practice! Why not have a go at the practice activities in this book that you haven't yet attempted? Once you have completed each task, ask someone to go through your answer with you and talk about your writing.

If you find any practice activity difficult, then look back through the relevant section in the book to remind yourself of the techniques that will help you to improve each aspect of your writing skills. For some more exam-style tasks, try the writing activities that are included in the two packs of *Bond 11⁺ Test Papers in English* (see the Additional resources appendix in section C (online) for more details). Remember that the more you practise, the better your writing will become.

Whether you have used this book because you will be sitting a writing exam paper soon or just to help support your general English skills, I wish you all the best and every success for the future.

Michellejoy

C Appendices

1 Practice activity extracts

Some of the practice activities in this book require children to read an extract before completing their task. Each of these extracts can be found in the online version of this appendix; see the Free Resources section for this book on the Bond website (www.bond11plus.co.uk).

2 Answers

1 Understand the task

Parent Note: A sample answer for each of the 22 writing prompts included in section B1 'Recognise the format', (pages 13–35) is available to download from our website: www.bond11plus.co.uk. Each sample answer is also supported by a tutor's commentary that explains the positive and negative aspects of the writing and offers suggestions for possible improvements. You may find it useful to compare these sample answers and comments to your child's own answers, so that you can talk together about the quality of their writing for each practice activity.

2 Improve your writing

Create a plan
Planning a narrative (page 57)
Nursery Rhymes – Line A: Little Bo–Peep; Line B: Humpty Dumpty; Line C: Pop goes the Weasel

Develop language skills
Include monosyllabic and polysyllabic words (practice activity, page 89)

1 syllable	2 syllables	3 syllables	4 syllables
rose	daisy	marigold	wisteria
weeds	holly	daffodil	honeysuckle
broom	tulip	conifer	loganberry
sprouts	crocus	tomatoes	celeriac
pears	grasses	ladybird	chrysanthemum
spade	carrots	millipede	asparagus
fork	parsnips	lettuces	Rotavator
hoe	apples	wheelbarrow	rhododendron
shed	ivy	mistletoe	geranium
pond	pumpkin	lavender	cauliflower

The word left over is escallonia; it has 5 syllables – es/ca/llo/ni/a.

Apply a wide vocabulary
(Practice activity for synonyms, page 91)
Possible answers: *enjoy, awful, excellent, friendly, interesting, first-rate, spacious, large*

(Practice activity for adverbs, page 96)
Possible answers: 1 *beautifully*   2 *peacefully*   3 *excitedly*   4 *erratically*   5 *silently*

Create the right image
(Practice activity for similes, page 102)

as pleased as punch	sing like a bird
as white as a sheet	sleep like a baby
as stubborn as a mule	swim like a fish
as wise as an owl	sweep into a room like a whirlwind

(Practice activity for personification, page 104)
Possible answers:
1 The cat *vaulted* on to the fence.   3 The wind *blew* the umbrella inside out.
2 The tractor *waddled* across the field.   4 The fruit bowl *sat* in the middle of the table.

(Practice activity for expressions, page 105)
1 Bob's your uncle   4 vanished into thin air
2 cheap at half the price   5 over the moon
3 your eyes are bigger than your stomach

(practice activity for proverbs, page 106)
1 Birds of a feather flock together.   d *People congregate with others who have similar interests.*

2 Nothing ventured, nothing gained.   f *You can't be rewarded for something if you don't try.*

3 Where there's a will there's a way.   b *If you really want to do something, you'll work out how to do it.*

4 Every cloud has a silver lining.   a *Something good will come out of even a very bad situation.*

5 A stitch in time saves nine.   c *It is better to do a job now, as it will only get worse later.*

6 Out of the frying pan, into the fire. e *You solve one bad situation and end up in one that is even worse.*

3 | Boost the basics

Grow your grammar

Sentences, phrases and clauses (page 117)
1 False.
2 A capital letter.
3 Two types of clause: a main clause; a subordinate clause.
4 True.
5 False.
6 A subordinate clause.
7 A verb.
8 A phrase.
9 True.

10 A sentence that is made up of more
than one clause or phrase.

11 A main clause.

12 Active.

Parts of speech (page 118)

1 d
2 Common noun: *crowd*; proper noun: *Jack*; abstract noun: *love*; collective noun: *bunch*.
3 True.
4 A verb is an action ('doing' or 'being') word that tells you what is happening to the subject in a sentence.
5 A noun.
6 How, where, when and how often something is happening.
7 a *behind*   b *during*   c *over*
8 They are used to join clauses or complete sentences together.
9 To be (or to have).
10 Simple: *large*   comparative: *larger*   superlative: *largest*
11 A proper noun.
12 The tense of a verb shows when the action of a sentence is happening.
13 4 types; personal: *she*   possessive: *mine*   relative: *which*   indefinite: *nothing*
14 False.
15 True.

Subjects and objects (page 118–119)

1 The subject of a sentence is who or what is doing the action of the verb in a sentence.
2 The object of a sentence is who or what is being affected by the subject and the verb in a sentence.
3 The verb.
4 False.
5 Common nouns, proper nouns or noun phrases.
6 a The Championship   b the beach   c puzzle book
7 Young Alice.

Practise your punctuation (pages 119–120)

1	,	(comma)	13	?	(question mark)
2	;	(semi-colon)	14	:	(colon)
3	-	(hyphen)	15	'	(apostrophe)
4	!	(exclamation mark)	16	...	(ellipsis)
5	:	(colon)	17	'	(apostrophe)
6	( )	(brackets)	18	"	(opening speech mark)
7	"	(closing speech mark)	19	!	(exclamation mark)
8		(paragraph)	20	;	(semi-colon)
9	.	(full stop)	21	,	(comma)
10	-	(hyphen)	22	,	(comma)
11	( )	(brackets)	23	w	(paragraph)
12	,	(comma)	24	–	(dash)

The **Bond** series offers extensive resources to support the development of your child's English skills:

✓ a complete course of workbooks that provide carefully graded, timed papers for extensive practice and revision
✓ mock test papers that present an authentic exam experience
✓ collections of short tests that offer essential bite-sized practice of all core skills
✓ workbooks that focus just on comprehension, providing extended practice of this vital skill
✓ tutorial guides that offer detailed strategies and practice activities for tackling all key topics and question types.

See the table below for individual title details.

BOND TITLES	ISBN
Bond English Assessment Papers 5–6 Years	978-0-7487-8464-6
Bond English Assessment Papers 6–7 Years	978-1-4085-1692-8
Bond English Assessment Papers 7–8 Years	978-1-4085-1689-8
Bond English Assessment Papers 8–9 Years	978-0-7487-8122-5
Bond English Assessment Papers 9–10 Years Book 1	978-1-4085-1625-6
Bond English Assessment Papers 9–10 Years Book 2	978-1-4085-1590-7
Bond English Assessment Papers 10–11$^+$ Years Book 1	978-1-4085-1586-0
Bond English Assessment Papers 10–11$^+$ Years Book 2	978-0-7487-8470-7
Bond English Assessment Papers 11$^+$–12$^+$ Years Book 1	978-1-4085-1630-1
Bond English Assessment Papers 11$^+$–12$^+$ Years Book 2	978-1-4085-1592-1
Bond English Assessment Papers 12$^+$–13$^+$ Years	978-1-4085-1607-2
11$^+$ Test Papers in English (Standard)	978-0-7487-8488-2
11$^+$ Test Papers in English (Multiple-choice)	978-0-7487-8487-5
11$^+$ Test Papers in English Pack 2 (Standard)	978-1-4085-0278-5
11$^+$ Test Papers in English Pack 2 (Multiple-choice)	978-1-4085-0277-8
10 Minute Tests in English 7–8 Years	978-1-4085-0262-4
10 Minute Tests in English 8–9 Years	978-1-4085-0266-2
10 Minute Tests in English 9–10 Years	978-0-7487-9896-4
10 Minute Tests in English 10–11$^+$ Years	978-0-7487-9697-7
10 Minute Tests in English 11$^+$–12$^+$ Years	978-0-7487-9900-8
Comprehension Third papers 9–10 Years	978-1-4085-0400-0
Comprehension Fourth papers 10–11$^+$ Years	978-1-4085-0401-7
Comprehension Fifth papers 11$^+$–12$^+$ Years	978-1-4085-0402-4
The secrets of Comprehension	978-0-7487-8480-6
How to do... 11$^+$ English	978-0-7487-9695-3
Get Ready for Secondary School: English	978-0-7487-7539-2
The Parents' Guide to the 11$^+$	978-1-4085-1582-2

A full range of materials is also available to support verbal reasoning, non-verbal reasoning and maths practice.

Bond No Nonsense (BNN) is a home learning series for 5–11-year-olds that provides clear and straightforward teaching and learning of maths and English.

BNN English TITLES	ISBN	BNN English TITLES	ISBN
Ages 5–6	978-0-7487-9562-8	Ages 8–9	978-0-7487-9565-9
Ages 6–7	978-0-7487-9563-5	Ages 9–10	978-0-7487-9566-6
Ages 7–8	978-0-7487-9564-2	Ages 10–11	978-0-7487-9567-3

Schonell's Essential Spelling series offers the *Essential Spelling List*, which includes over 3000 words that children often need to use in writing tasks, and three *Essential Spelling* workbooks for additional practice of keywords.

SCHONELL'S TITLES	ISBN	SCHONELL'S TITLES	ISBN
The Essential Spelling List	978-0-17-424493-6	The Essential Spelling Book 2	978-0-17-424082-2
The Essential Spelling Bk 1	978-0-17-424083-9	The Essential Spelling Book 3	978-0-17-424081-5

For more details on any of these titles, please visit www.bond11plus.co.uk.